THE
SALSA
IS
HOT

Dialogs & Stories

WILLIAM P. PICKETT

Passaic High School

Longman

Pickett, William P.
    The salsa is hot: dialogs and stories / William P. Pickett
        p.   cm.
    Includes index.
    ISBN 0-13-020436-6
    1. English language– –Textbooks for foreign speakers.   2. Readers.
  I. Title.
PE1128.P484 1999   98-49581
428.2'4– –dc21   CIP

Acquisitions Editor: *Sheryl Olinsky*
Development Editor: *Pamela Renner*
AVP/Director of Production and Manufacturing: *Aliza Greenblatt*
Executive Managing Editor: *Dominick Mosco*
Art Director/Cover Designer: *Merle Krumper*
Electronic Publishing Specialist: *Steven Greydanus*
Manufacturing Manager: *Dave Dickey*
Illustrator: *Don Martinetti*

© 1999 by PRENTICE HALL REGENTS
A Pearson Education Company
Pearson Education, 10 Bank Street, White Plains, NY 10606

Reprinted with corrections September, 1999.

Printed in the United States of America
10 9 8 7 6 5 4

0-13-020436-6

To my brothers,
John and Ray,
and my sister,
Mary Jane

Contents

Preface   viii

Acknowledgements   x

 **Jobs**   1

    Good Tips   2
    Baby-Sitting   5
    A Police Officer   8
    Delivering Mail   11
      From Quito to Jersey City   14
      Working in a Diner   18

Sports   23

    Basketball or Math   24
    Football   27
    Hunting   30
    A Hockey Star   33
      Roberto Clemente   36
      The Hall of Fame   40

Celebrations   45

    The Fourth of July   46
    Trick or Treat   49
    Turkey Day   52
    Birthday Presents   55
      The Pilgrims   58
      A Soldier   62

Love   67

The Big Dance   68

The Matchmaker   71

A Lot in Common   74

Valentine's Day   77

   Hard at First   80

   A Diamond Ring   84

 Dogs and Money   89

Man's Best Friend   90

Feeling Lucky   93

A Big Shot   96

New Furniture   99

   Very Different   102

   Mark, Emily, and Midnight   106

 Food   111

I'm Starving   112

More Chicken!   115

The Salsa Is Hot   118

The C.I.A.   121

   A Store and a Home   124

   Growing Up in America   128

7 Cars and Accidents 133

An Accident   134

911   137

Quiet, Roomy, and Safe   140

The Ax Slipped   143

The Titanic   146

Iceberg Ahead   150

8 School 155

The First Day of School   156

Old-Fashioned   159

Writing Is Tough Work   162

A Million Rules   165

More Opportunities   168

A Dream Come True   172

Irregular Verbs 177

Maps 178

Word List 180

Preface

OVERVIEW

The Salsa Is Hot is a reader featuring thirty-three dialogs and seven stories about events in the lives of a number of ordinary people and of a few famous ones. The book is about people: their joys and struggles, their hopes and fears, their light moments and their serious ones.

Above all, the book aims to be interesting, one that students will enjoy while improving their reading and conversational skills.

Most of the stories are about newcomers to the United States, people from Ecuador, Puerto Rico, Poland, India, and Haiti. One story is about the Pilgrims and the Native Americans who helped them. The dialogs also feature people from many cultures.

LEVEL

The Salsa is written for advanced beginners who have a basic vocabulary and have already done some easy reading. At the same time, vocabulary and structures are controlled so the students can understand and enjoy what they are reading.

OBJECTIVES

The Salsa Is Hot was designed to
- provide interesting reading material and improve reading skills,
- increase vocabulary,
- improve listening comprehension, and
- increase fluency through discussions and roleplaying.

AUDIENCE

This book is written for adults of all ages. It can be used successfully in two- and four-year colleges and high schools, in adult education classes, and for home study.

CONTENTS

A. Word Bank

All the dialogs and stories in *The Salsa Is Hot* are preceded by a Word Bank that defines the more difficult words the student will encounter. Each definition is accompanied by an example sentence that helps clarify the definition.

Since the Word Bank is a glossary, it usually includes only the meaning each word has in the dialog or story. Note that sometimes this is not the most common meaning of the word.

If the Word Bank gives two definitions for a word and these definitions are basically the same, a *semicolon* separates them. When the definitions are different, which is rare, a *colon* separates them.

Although the Word Bank is placed before the dialog or story, teachers and students may prefer to use it *after* reading the dialog or story. Teachers are encouraged to experiment to see which order best suits their teaching style and the learning styles of their students. To indicate that the glossary can be used after reading the dialog or story as well as before, its name was changed from Word Preview to Word Bank.

B. Preview Questions

The dialogs and stories of *The Salsa* are preceded by questions designed to stimulate a student's curiosity and prior knowledge of the topic of the dialog or story.

C. Dialogs and Stories

Every chapter of this book, except chapter three, contains four dialogs and a story about topics such as jobs, sports, love, food, and school. The dialogs are about 14 lines in length and can be used for roleplaying as well as for reading. The stories are about 200 words long and are more difficult than the dialogs because their sentences are longer and their structures are more formal.

D. Comprehension Questions

Comprehension questions immediately follow all the dialogs and stories. Many of the questions are factual, but some require students to go beyond the text and make inferences or give opinions. Some of the dialogs are followed by true-false questions.

E. Sharing Information

A Sharing Information section follows the comprehension questions. This section encourages students to converse freely about topics related to the dialogs and stories. It gives students the opportunity to express their ideas, feelings, and opinions, and to increase their fluency.

F. Sentence Completion, Story Completion, Matching, and Dictation

A sentence-completion, story-completion, or matching exercise usually follows the Sharing Information section. These exercises reinforce and test the vocabulary used in the dialogs and stories. After the first dialog of every chapter, a dictation exercise follows the Sharing Information section.

G. True-False Questions, Synonyms, and Antonyms

Every chapter ends with true-false questions and a synonym and antonym exercise in which the vocabulary of the chapter is reviewed.

H. Irregular Verbs, Maps, and Word List

In the back of the book is an alphabetical listing of the irregular verbs used in the past tense. There are also maps of Puerto Rico, the Dominican Republic and Haiti, Ecuador, Poland, and India. People from these countries are featured in *The Salsa*. Finally, there is a list of all the words defined in the Word Bank.

REVIEW TESTS, ANSWER KEY, AND AUDIOCASSETTE

A separate booklet contains review tests for the eight chapters of *The Salsa* as well as an answer key for these tests and for the exercises in *The Salsa*. An audiocassette with all the dialogs and stories is also available.

THREE-LEVEL SERIES

The Pizza Tastes Great, The Salsa Is Hot, and *The Chicken Smells Good* form a series. *The Pizza* is written for beginners, *The Salsa* for advanced beginners, and *The Chicken* for low intermediates. The hallmark of the series is its combination of interesting dialogs and stories about people with whom the students can identify. Students enjoy reading and talking about these stories and dialogs and learn a lot from them.

ACKNOWLEDGEMENTS

I wish to thank everyone at Prentice Hall Regents who helped in the publication of *The Salsa*. I am especially grateful to Sheryl Olinsky, my editor, to Pamela Renner, my development editor, and to Christine Mann, my production editor. All made special contributions to *The Salsa*, and I greatly appreciate their assistance.

I also wish to thank Don Martinetti, who did the art work. His excellent illustrations capture the spirit of the dialogs and stories.

Above all, I am grateful to my wife, Dorothy, who spent so much time going over all the dialogs and stories. Many of her suggestions are incorporated in the book, and *The Salsa* is much better for them.

1

Jobs

Good Tips

WORD BANK

1. **customer** *n.* a person who buys something "Lauren buys a lot of things in our store. She's a good <u>customer</u>."
2. **friendly** *adj.* acting like a friend; nice "Dan says hello to everyone. He's <u>friendly</u>."
3. **imagine** *v.* to form an idea or picture of something in one's mind "The children didn't have breakfast. I can <u>imagine</u> how hungry they are."
4. **low** *adj.* less than usual "My apartment is small. That's why the rent is <u>low</u>."
5. **polite** *adj.* having good manners; showing respect to others "John opened the door and let me go into the room first. He's <u>polite</u>."
6. **tip** *n.* or *v.* extra money we give to waitresses (waiters), barbers, and taxi drivers "The taxi driver is hoping for a big <u>tip</u>."
7. **too** *adv.* also "I speak Italian, and my brother does <u>too</u>."
8. **tough** *adj.* not easy; difficult "It's <u>tough</u> to work for Mr. Grant. He's always checking on everyone."
9. **waitress** *n.* a woman who serves people at a restaurant "The <u>waitress</u> is bringing our dinner."
10. **why** *idiom* an informal expression showing surprise (*Why* usually introduces a question, but not in this dialog.) "Karol is going to Poland this summer." "<u>Why</u>, that's great."

PREVIEW QUESTIONS

Discuss these questions before reading the dialog.

1. Why is it hard to be a waiter or waitress?
2. Many waiters and waitresses make good money, but their salaries are low. How is that possible?

    Ling is studying computer science at a community college. She also works as a waitress in a Chinese restaurant. She's talking to Ahmad, who goes to the same community college.

Ahmad: Where are you going?

Ling: To work. I'm a waitress at a Chinese restaurant.

Ahmad: Do you like it?

Ling: Yes, but it's tough work.

Ahmad: I can imagine.

Ling: I'm on my feet for seven hours.

Ahmad: And how's the pay?

Ling: It's low, but I get good tips.

Ahmad: The customers must like you.

Ling: They do. I'm always friendly and polite.

Ahmad: And you're smart too.

Ling: Why, thank you.

COMPREHENSION

Answer these questions about the dialog. Use your own ideas to answer questions with an asterisk. (* = asterisk)

1. What is Ling's job?
2. Is her job easy?
3. How long is she on her feet?
4. How is her pay?
5. What do the customers give her?
6. Why do they like her?
*7. How much do you think Ling makes a day in tips?

SHARING INFORMATION

Discuss these questions in pairs or small groups.

1. How much do people usually tip waiters and waitresses?
2. Who else do we usually tip?
3. Why do we tip these people?
4. Do you think that most waiters and waitresses are polite?

DICTATION

1. Listen while the teacher reads the dialog without stopping. <u>Don't write anything</u>.

2. The teacher will read the dialog a second time, pausing after the missing lines. <u>Write in the missing lines</u>.

3. The teacher will read the dialog a third time. <u>Check your work</u>.

Ahmad: Where are you going?

Ling: _____

Ahmad: Do you like it?

Ling: _____

Ahmad: I can imagine.

Ling: _____

Ahmad: And how's the pay?

Ling: _____

Ahmad: The customers must like you.

Ling: _____

Baby-Sitting

1. **a lot** *idiom* much "Audrey doesn't eat <u>a lot</u>. That's why she's thin."
2. **allow** *v.* to let someone do something "They don't <u>allow</u> dogs in these apartments."
3. **baby-sit** *v.* to take care of another person's baby "Mr. and Mrs. Fisher are going out tonight. The girl who lives across the street is going to <u>baby-sit</u> for them."
4. **besides** *adv.* in addition; what's more "Larry is going to bed. He's tired. <u>Besides</u>, he has to get up early tomorrow."
5. **better (than)** *adj.* the comparative of *good* "I don't like this bike. I'm going to buy a <u>better</u> one."
6. **boring** *adj.* not interesting "No one likes our history class. It's <u>boring</u>."
7. **company** *n.* people who come to visit "We're having <u>company</u> tonight. That's why we're cleaning the house."
8. **have got to** *idiom* must "My car won't start. I <u>have got to</u> take a taxi to work."
9. **later** *adv.* comparative of *late* "We're not hungry now. We'll eat <u>later</u>."
10. **lose** *v.* to have something and not be able to keep it "If you're not polite to your customers, you'll <u>lose</u> them."
11. **so** *adv.* very "I like Jean. She's <u>so</u> nice."
12. **sorry** *adj.* feeling unhappy about something "We're <u>sorry</u> we can't help you now. We're very busy."
13. **understand** *v.* to know well "I <u>understand</u> the plan, and I think it's a good one."
14. **wrong** *adj.* not right; bad "There's nothing <u>wrong</u> with Vicky. She feels fine."

PREVIEW QUESTIONS

Discuss these questions before reading the dialog.

1. What do baby sitters usually do?
2. Do they get much money? How much do you think they should get an hour?

Ken and Pam are high-school seniors. Ken wants to take Pam out tonight, but she can't go. She has to baby-sit.

Ken: Do you want to go to a dance tonight?

Pam: I'm sorry. I can't. Some other night.

Ken: What's wrong with tonight?

Pam: I've got to baby-sit.

Ken: Baby-sit? Isn't that boring?

Pam: It's not so bad. Besides, I need the money.

Ken: How much do you get?

Pam: Five dollars an hour.

Ken: That's not a lot.

Pam: I know, but it's better than nothing.

Ken: Can I come over and keep you company?

Pam: No, Mrs. Franco doesn't allow that. And I don't want to lose my job.

Ken: I understand. See you later.

TRUE OR FALSE

If the sentence is true, write T. *If it's false, write* F.

_____ 1. Pam is going to a dance.

_____ 2. She has to work.

_____ 3. She is rich.

_____ 4. She is going to make a lot of money.

_____ 5. Ken wants to visit Pam.

_____ 6. Mrs. Franco doesn't want anyone to stay with Pam.

SHARING INFORMATION

Discuss these questions in pairs or small groups.

1. How old should one be before he or she baby-sits?
2. What kind of person do parents look for when they choose a baby sitter?
3. Do you think baby-sitting is an easy job? Explain your answer.
4. Do you think it's boring? Explain your answer.

STORY COMPLETION

Eric Can't Play in the Big Game

Eric is a very good baseball player, but he can't play in today's big game because he's sick.

Complete the story with these words.

besides	later	wrong	better
has got to	allow	boring	sorry

Eric is one of the _____ players on his baseball team, but his parents won't _____ him to play in this morning's big game.

His parents are _____ they can't let him play, but he's sick and they don't know what's _____ with him. He _____ stay home. They're going to bring him to see a doctor _____ today.

Eric isn't happy. He wants to play. It's _____ to stay home when everyone else is at the game. _____, his team needs him.

A Police Officer

WORD BANK

1. **dad** (informal) *n.* a father   "Ed and Jessica are going to the park with their <u>dad</u>."
2. **dangerous** *adj.* anything that can easily hurt someone   "Driving in snow can be <u>dangerous</u>."
3. **have to** *idiom* must; to be necessary   "I'm very tired. I <u>have to</u> go to bed."
4. **kid** *v.* to joke (A person who *kids* is not serious.)   "Vanessa was only <u>kidding</u> when she said she got 100 on her math test. She got 70."
5. **like** *prep.* for example   "For Tom's birthday, I'm going to get him something he'll wear, <u>like</u> a sweater or a jacket."
6. **of course** *idiom* naturally; clearly   "<u>Of course</u>, I want to go to the parade. I love parades."
7. **police officer** *n.* a policeman or policewoman   "A <u>police officer</u> stopped me because I was driving too fast."
8. **still** *adv.* continuing to   "Is Rita <u>still</u> sleeping?"

PREVIEW QUESTIONS

Discuss these questions before reading the dialog.

1. What's the big problem with being a police officer?
2. Has a police officer ever helped you? How?

Tamika is 21 years old. She's telling her father she wants to be a police officer. He's not happy about it.

Tamika: Dad, I have something to tell you.

Dad: What is it?

Tamika: I want to be a police officer.

Dad: A what?

Tamika: A police officer.

Dad: Are you kidding?

Tamika: No, I'm very serious, Dad.

Dad: Do you know how dangerous that is?

Tamika: Of course, I do. I'm 21. I'm not a child.

Dad: Why don't you be something safe, like a nurse or a lawyer?

Tamika: I don't want to be a nurse or a lawyer.

Dad: Fine. But why a police officer?

Tamika: Dad, it's my life. You have to let me try.

Dad: OK. But I'm still not happy about it.

COMPREHENSION

Answer these questions about the dialog. Use your own ideas to answer questions with an asterisk.

1. What does Tamika want to be?
2. Is she kidding?
3. Why doesn't Tamika's dad want her to be a police officer?
4. How old is Tamika?
5. What does her dad want her to be?
6. What does she say her dad has to do?
*7. What do you think Tamika's mother is going to say when Tamika tells her that she wants to be a police officer?

SHARING INFORMATION

Discuss these questions in pairs or small groups.

1. If you wanted to be a police officer, would your family be happy? Explain your answer.
2. Police officers have to go to a special school before they start work. Why?
3. Do you think most police officers like to help people?
4. Does the city in which you live have bilingual police officers? Do you think they need more?

SENTENCE COMPLETION

Complete the sentences with these words.

still	police officer	dangerous	kidding	let

1. It's _____ to play in the street.
2. That's why I don't _____ my children play in the street.
3. Is the food _____ hot?
4. Bob says he's moving to Texas, and he isn't _____.
5. A _____ is directing traffic.

safe	have to	of course	serious	like

6. I'm happy that the accident wasn't _____.
7. The park is _____ during the day.
8. _____, I'll help you. What do you want?
9. Eat something that's good for you, _____ an apple or an orange.
10. I _____ talk to you. Do you have a minute?

Delivering Mail

1. **apply** *v.* to ask for something formally and in writing, for example, to apply for a job "Abdul is <u>applying</u> for a visa to visit his county."
2. **bet** *v.* to be sure or almost sure "I <u>bet</u> the children want ice cream."
3. **bother** *v.* to disturb; to give people attention they don't want. "George is studying for a big test. Don't <u>bother</u> him."
4. **deliver** *v.* to bring something to a home or business, for example, a package "They're going to <u>deliver</u> the computer to my house tomorrow."
5. **fire** *v.* to take a job away from someone "If you're late for work again, the company is going to <u>fire</u> you."
6. **hate** *v.* or *n.* to dislike very much (*Hate* is the opposite of *love*.) "Angela loves to eat, but she <u>hates</u> to cook."
7. **letter carrier** *n.* a post office worker who brings letters to people's homes "Did the <u>letter carrier</u> come yet?"
8. **outdoors** *adv.* out of a house or other building "We should spend more time <u>outdoors</u>."
9. **rush** *v.* or *n.* to move fast; to cause a person to move fast "Andy's mother is <u>rushing</u> him. She doesn't want him to be late for school."
10. **secure** *adj.* safe "I want my money to be <u>secure</u>. That's why I put it in the bank and leave it there."

PREVIEW QUESTIONS

Discuss these questions before reading the dialog.

1. Do you think a letter carrier has an interesting job? Explain your answer.
2. Do you think a letter carrier has a hard job? Explain your answer.

Doug works for the U.S. Post Office. He's a letter carrier. He's talking to his friend Ashley about his job.

Ashley: Do you like being a letter carrier?

Doug: It's not bad, and the pay is good.

Ashley: How do you like working outdoors?

Doug: I love it.

Ashley: But I bet you don't like rain or snow.

Doug: Rain is not so bad, but I hate snow.

Ashley: Do dogs bother you much?

Doug: No, I like dogs.

Ashley: What's the best thing about your job?

Doug: It's secure. No one is going to fire me.

Ashley: True—they always need someone to deliver the mail.

Doug: And another good thing. No one rushes you.

Ashley: Maybe I should apply for a job at the post office.

Doug: Sure. Why not?

TRUE OR FALSE

If the sentence is true, write T. *If it's false, write* F.

_____   1. Doug usually likes working outdoors.

_____   2. He doesn't like snow.

_____   3. Dogs are a big problem for him.

_____   4. He worries about losing his job.

_____   5. His boss wants him to work faster.

_____   6. Ashley is thinking about applying for a job at the post office.

SHARING INFORMATION

Discuss these questions in pairs or small groups.

1. Name some good and bad things about being a letter carrier.
2. Would you like to be a letter carrier? Why or why not?
3. A letter carrier's job is secure. Name some other secure jobs.
4. Which do you think is better—a secure job with a good salary, or a job that isn't secure, but with a *very* good salary? Explain your answer.

MATCHING

Match the words in Column A with their definitions or descriptions in Column B. Print the letters on the blank lines.

Column A	Column B
_____ 1. allow	A. also
_____ 2. still	B. extra money
_____ 3. tough	C. safe
_____ 4. too	D. to move fast
_____ 5. bother	E. to let
_____ 6. secure	F. visitors
_____ 7. company	G. difficult
_____ 8. tip	H. unhappy about something
_____ 9. sorry	I. continuing to
_____ 10. rush	J. to disturb

From Quito to Jersey City

WORD BANK

1. **ago** *adv.* in the past "Donna isn't here. She went to school ten minutes <u>ago</u>."
2. **discover** *v.* to learn; to come to know "I <u>discovered</u> that my friend had a lot of money in the bank."
3. **engaged** *adj.* having an agreement to marry "Heather and Brian are <u>engaged</u>. They're going to get married in June."
4. **equator** *n.* an imaginary line around the middle of the earth "It is usually very hot at the <u>equator</u>."
5. **few** *adj.* a small number of "It's ten o'clock. We have to leave in a <u>few</u> minutes."
6. **find** *v.* to look for and get "Emily is looking for her watch. I hope she <u>finds</u> it."
7. **help-wanted ad** *n.* a notice placed in a newspaper to offer and give information about a job (*Ad* is short for *advertisement*.) "Ben is looking for work. That's why he reads the <u>help-wanted ads</u> every day."
8. **hire** *v.* to give a job to; to employ "The factory <u>hired</u> 20 more workers."
9. **humid** *adj.* having a lot of water in the air "We get a lot of <u>humid</u> weather in the summer."
10. **peaceful** *adj.* quiet; calm "It's very <u>peaceful</u> where we live."
11. **smile** *n.* or *v.* the act of smiling (To *smile* is to show that you are happy by turning up the corners of your lips.) "I'm ready to take your picture. <u>Smile</u>, please."
12. **soon** *adv.* in a short time "The letter carrier will be here <u>soon</u>."

PREVIEW QUESTIONS

Discuss these questions before reading the story.

1. Quito is the capital of Ecuador, and *ecuador* is the Spanish word for equator. What is the equator?
2. Why do most immigrants come to the United States?
3. Do you think it is easy to get a job in the United States? Explain your answer.

Juan Velez is from Quito, the capital of Ecuador. Quito is only a few miles from the equator, but it's in the mountains and never gets hot. It's a pretty city and very peaceful.

Juan came to the United States a year ago because he couldn't find a job in Quito. He was 21 and engaged to Sonia Reyes, a girl with beautiful black hair and the nicest smile. It wasn't easy to leave Sonia and his family, but Juan hoped to make a lot of money in the United States.

Juan left Ecuador in the beginning of July, and his first month in the United States was very difficult. He lived with his cousin in a small apartment in Jersey City. The weather was hot and humid, and his room didn't have air conditioning.

Juan didn't have much education and knew only a few words of English. He soon discovered that it wasn't easy to get a job. He visited some factories, but they weren't hiring. He looked at the help-wanted ads in the Spanish newspaper, but there was nothing for him. Juan talked to his cousin; he couldn't help. But Juan continued to look for work.

COMPREHENSION

Answer these questions about the story. Use your own ideas to answer questions with an asterisk.

Paragraph 1
1. Why doesn't it get hot in Quito?
2. Describe Quito.

Paragraph 2
3. Why did Juan Velez come to the United States?
4. Who is he going to marry? Describe her.
5. What did he hope to do in the United States?
*6. Do most immigrants think they're going to make a lot money in the United States? Explain your answer.

Paragraph 3
7. Where did Juan live when he came to the United States?
8. What was the problem with the weather in Jersey City?
*9. Do you think July was a good month for Juan to come to the United States? Explain your answer.

Paragraph 4
10. How much English did Juan know?
11. What did he soon discover?
12. Name three things he did to find a job.

SHARING INFORMATION

Discuss these questions in pairs or small groups.

1. What country are you from?
2. What city? What is its population? Describe its weather.
3. How long ago did you come to the United States?
4. Why did you come?
5. What problems did you have your first month here?
6. Was the weather a problem? If so, why?
7. How much English did you know when you came to the United States?

STORY COMPLETION

Getting Married

Amanda and I met at a picnic, and I liked her a lot. Ten months later, we decided to get married. We want to buy a house before we get married.

Complete the story with these words.

discovered	find	favorite	smile
few	soon	ago	engaged

A year _____, I met Amanda at a picnic. She was very nice and had a pretty _____. I also _____ that she liked to play tennis, my _____ sport.

We were _____ playing tennis when we could and going to the movies. Ten months later, we got _____. We're going to get married in a _____ months.

Amanda and I plan to buy a house before we get married. We have looked at many houses, but we still can't _____ the one we want.

Working in a Diner

1. **along** *prep.* by the side of "They're planting trees <u>along</u> the highway."
2. **arrive** *v.* to come to a place "What time did you <u>arrive</u> home?"
3. **at least** *idiom* if nothing more; if nothing else "I don't like our new boss, but <u>at least</u> she listens to people."
4. **diner** *n.* a restaurant with a large menu, low prices, and fast service "I'm hungry. Let's stop at the <u>diner</u>."
5. **enough** *adj.*, *adv.*, or *pron.* as much as needed "Do we have <u>enough</u> food for the picnic?"
6. **expensive** *adj.* costing a lot of money "That's a nice coat. I bet it's <u>expensive</u>."
7. **finally** *adv.* happening after a long wait "The bus <u>finally</u> came."
8. **immigrant** *n.* a person who comes from another country to live here "<u>Immigrants</u> come to the United States from all parts of the world."
9. **miss** *v.* to feel bad because someone you love is not with you "Ellen's husband is in Chicago for a week. She <u>misses</u> him."
10. **remind** *v.* to cause a person to remember "The photo <u>reminded</u> me of my trip to San Francisco."
11. **so** *conj.* in order to; with the purpose of "Sharon is buying a computer <u>so</u> she can work at home."
12. **soccer** *n.* a game in which you advance the ball by kicking it—this game is called *football* in most countries "<u>Soccer</u> is the most popular sport in the world."
13. **view** *n.* or *v.* what we see at a distance, especially something beautiful "There is a great <u>view</u> of the park from our hotel room."

PREVIEW QUESTIONS

Discuss these questions before reading the story.

1. They say that the United States is a country of immigrants. What does that mean?
2. How often do you write to friends and relatives in your country?
3. How often do you phone them? How expensive is it?

Juan finally got a job working in the kitchen at Bill's Diner on Kennedy Boulevard in Jersey City. The kitchen is hot, and it's a tough job. Juan doesn't make a lot of money, but at least he has a job. He's making enough to pay his bills and save a little.

Juan's life isn't all work and no play. On Sundays, he goes with his cousin and some friends to Liberty State Park. They have a picnic and play soccer, their favorite sport.

After the game, they walk along the Hudson River where there is a beautiful view of the Statue of Liberty[1] and Ellis Island.[2] The statue and the island remind Juan that he lives in a country of immigrants—that this is his land, too.

Juan phones Sonia every Sunday. The calls are expensive, but he hates to write, and he has to talk to her. He misses her so much.

Juan and Sonia plan to marry a year from now. She'll fly to the United States, and they'll get married here. He's saving every penny he can so they can rent a nice apartment. And Sonia is studying English so she can get a good job when she arrives.

---

1. The **Statue of Liberty** is a large statue of a woman, the symbol of liberty. The statue is on an island in New York Harbor and is a gift from France. The Statue of Liberty was the first thing many immigrants saw as they sailed into New York Harbor from Europe.
2. **Ellis Island** is a small island in New York Harbor where ships brought immigrants before they were let into the United States. Doctors checked the immigrants, and those with certain sicknesses were sent back to their countries. Today Ellis Island is open to the public, and many people visit it.

COMPREHENSION

Answer these questions about the story. Use your own ideas to answer questions with an asterisk.

Paragraph 1
1. Where does Juan work?
2. What does he do with the money he makes?

Paragraph 2
3. Where does Juan go on Sunday?
4. What does he do there?

Paragraph 3
5. What do Juan and his friends do after they play soccer?
6. What does he remember when he sees the Statue of Liberty and Ellis Island?
*7. Why do you think the government stopped using Ellis Island to receive immigrants?

Paragraph 4
8. Why does Juan phone Sonia every Sunday?
*9. When do phone calls cost less? Why?

Paragraph 5
10. When do Juan and Sonia plan to get married?
11. Why is he saving every penny he can?
12. Why is she studying English?

SHARING INFORMATION

Discuss these questions in pairs or small groups.

1. Name as many jobs as you can in which you don't need English.
2. Do those jobs pay well?
3. What do you do to relax and have fun?
4. Do you go to a park often? If so, why do you go?
5. Do you have a favorite sport? What is it?
6. Who do you miss the most from your country?
7. Do you work? If so, where?
8. What job would you like to have some day?

SENTENCE COMPLETION

Complete the sentences with these words.

expensive	diner	rent	enough	finally

1. We don't have _____ time to go to the movies.
2. It's _____ to fly.
3. How much will it cost to _____ a car for a week?
4. Joan and Paul _____ got married.
5. The _____ has very good fish.

view	arrive	so	miss	at least

6. Alex is staying home _____ he can study.
7. It's a cloudy day, but _____ it isn't raining.
8. I love the _____ from the top of the mountain.
9. Our daughter is getting married next month. We're going to
   _____ her.
10. I'm waiting for the mail to _____. I expect an
    important letter.

TRUE OR FALSE

If the sentence is true, write T. *If it's false, write* F *and change it to a true statement.*

_____ 1. Taxi drivers love tips.

_____ 2. It's expensive to eat at a diner.

_____ 3. Letter carriers work outdoors a lot.

_____ 4. Some teachers are boring.

_____ 5. It's dangerous to be a waitress.

_____ 6. Few children like ice cream.

_____ 7. Lazy people hate to work.

SYNONYMS

Synonyms are words that have the same or a similar meaning. Next to each sentence, write a synonym for the underlined word or words.

a lot	kid	of course	soon
so	dad	have got to	understand

1. The play is going to start <u>in a short time</u>. _____
2. My <u>father</u> is a dentist. _____
3. The baby doesn't cry <u>much</u>. _____
4. <u>Naturally</u>, I want you to stop smoking. _____
5. Your garden is <u>very</u> pretty. _____
6. I <u>must</u> return these books to the library. _____
7. Doris is usually serious, but she also likes to <u>joke</u>. _____
8. I <u>know</u> what you're saying. _____

ANTONYMS

Antonyms are words that have opposite meanings. In the blank spaces, write an antonym for each word.

better	fire	hate	wrong
arrive	dangerous	few	boring

1. many _____
2. hire _____
3. leave _____
4. interesting _____
5. love _____
6. worse _____
7. safe _____
8. right _____

2

Sports

Basketball or Math

WORD BANK

1. **hard** *adv.* or *adj.* with a lot of effort "Cynthia works <u>hard</u>."
2. **homework** *n.* schoolwork that a student must do at home "Our science teacher gives us a lot of <u>homework</u>."
3. **lucky** *adj.* having good luck; fortunate (*Luck* is what happens to a person by chance. It is something one cannot control.) "Mike was in a bad accident. He's <u>lucky</u> he's OK."
4. **tired** *adj.* needing rest or sleep "You're <u>tired</u>. Why don't you sit down and rest?"
5. **too** *adv.* more than is good or necessary "That suit is <u>too</u> expensive. I can't buy it."
6. **worry** *v.* or *n.* to be afraid that something bad happened or may happen "Sara doesn't look well. I <u>worry</u> about her."

PREVIEW QUESTIONS

Discuss these questions before reading the dialog.

1. Is there a park near your home?
2. Describe the park.

 Kristin is going to the park to play basketball. Brenda can't come. She has to study for a math test.

Brenda: Where are you going?

Kristin: To the park.

Brenda: Why?

Kristin: To play basketball. Do you want to come?

Brenda: I would like to, but I can't.

Kristin: Why not?

Brenda: I have to study for my math test. It's going to be tough.

Kristin: You can study later.

Brenda: No, I'll be too tired. Do you have any homework?

Kristin: Not tonight.

Brenda: You're lucky.

Kristin: I know. See you later. Don't study too hard.

Brenda: Don't worry. I won't.

COMPREHENSION

Answer these questions about the dialog. Use your own ideas to answer questions with an asterisk.

1. Why is Kristin going to the park?
2. Why can't Brenda play basketball?
3. When does Kristin want Brenda to study?
4. Why can't Brenda study later?
5. Does Kristin have any homework?
6. What does Brenda say about Kristin?
*7. Do you think Brenda is a serious student? Explain your answer.

SHARING INFORMATION

Discuss these questions in pairs or small groups.

1. Do you like basketball? Do you ever watch it on TV? Often?
2. Do you ever play basketball? Often?
3. Do you like math?
4. Do you think it's a tough subject? Are you good at it?

DICTATION

1. *Listen while the teacher reads the dialog without stopping. Don't write anything.*

2. *The teacher will read the dialog a second time, pausing after the missing lines. Write in the missing lines.*

3. *The teacher will read the dialog a third time. Check your work.*

Kristin: I'm going to the park to play basketball. Do you want to come?

Brenda: _____

Kristin: Why not?

Brenda: _____

Kristin: You can study later.

Brenda: _____

Kristin: Not tonight.

Brenda: _____

Kristin: I know. See you later. Don't study too hard.

Brenda: _____

Football

WORD BANK

1. **back** *n.* a position on a football team (*Backs* often run with the ball.) "Pete is the best <u>back</u> on our football team. He's very fast."
2. **cross** *v.* to go from one side to the other "We used a boat to <u>cross</u> the river."
3. **go ahead** *idiom* to begin to do something "I think you have a good plan. <u>Go ahead</u> with it."
4. **hurt** *v.* to injure part of the body "Two people got <u>hurt</u> in the car accident. They're in the hospital."
5. **pound** *n.* unit of weight = .454 kilogram (*Weight* is a measure of how heavy a person or thing is.) "I'm going to get five <u>pounds</u> of sugar."
6. **weigh** *v.* to have a certain weight "Frank is thin. He <u>weighs</u> only 120 pounds."

PREVIEW QUESTIONS

Discuss these questions before reading the dialog.

1. What are the most popular sports in your country?
2. What do you know about American football? Do you like the game? Do you ever watch it on TV? Often?

Tony wants to play football, but his mother thinks it's too dangerous. She wants him to play a safe game, like soccer.

Tony: Mom, I want to play football.

Mom: I'm sorry, but you can't.

Tony: Why not? I love football.

Mom: It's too dangerous. You can get hurt easily.

Tony: Yes, and I can get hurt crossing the street.

Mom: That's different. How much do you weigh?

Tony: 155 pounds.

Mom: You're not big enough to play football.

Tony: I don't have to be big. I'm a back, and I'm very fast.

Mom: Why don't you play a safe game, like soccer?

Tony: It's not my game. Mom, please let me play football!

Mom: OK, OK! Go ahead. You can play.

Tony: Thanks, Mom. You're the greatest.

Mom: But be careful!

Tony: Don't worry, Mom. I won't get hurt.

TRUE OR FALSE

If the sentence is true, write T. *If it's false, write* F.

_____   1. Tony wants to play basketball.

_____   2. His mother is afraid to let him play football.

_____   3. Tony got hurt crossing the street.

_____   4. He's not big, but he's very fast.

_____   5. He loves to play soccer.

_____   6. His mother decides to let him play football.

SHARING INFORMATION

Discuss these questions in pairs or small groups.

1. What are some of the good things about playing sports?
2. Football is dangerous. Name some other dangerous sports.
3. Name some safe sports.
4. Do you have a favorite professional football team, for example, the New York Giants or the Dallas Cowboys?

STORY COMPLETION

A Lot of Vegetables

Janet eats a lot and doesn't get much exercise. She's afraid of having a heart attack. She plans to go on a diet.

Complete the story with these words.

pounds	**worries**	**too**	**dangerous**
goes ahead	**enough**	**like**	**weighs**

My friend Janet has a problem. She eats _____ much and doesn't get _____ exercise. That's why she _____ 180 _____.

Janet knows this can be _____, and sometimes she _____ about having a heart attack.

She plans to go on a diet and to eat a lot of vegetables, _____ carrots, peas, and broccoli. But before she _____ with her diet, she's going to see her doctor.

Hunting

1. **beef** *n.* the meat of a cow or bull   "The hamburgers are all <u>beef</u>."
2. **believe in** *v.* to think that something is good—that it has value   "I don't <u>believe in</u> hitting children."
3. **deer** *n.* a large animal that has four thin legs, is fast, and very beautiful   "Be quiet or the <u>deer</u> will run away."
4. **exercise** *n.* or *v.* physical activity, for example, walking or running   "I often walk in the park. It's good <u>exercise</u>."
5. **fresh** *adj.* clean and cool   "Open the window and let in some <u>fresh</u> air."
6. **fun** *n.* pleasure; a good time   "We had <u>fun</u> at the party."
7. **hunt** *v.* or *n.* to look for animals to kill or capture   "Roger and Tyler are <u>hunting</u> for rabbits."
8. **just** *adv.* only; nothing more than   "I <u>just</u> work here. I'm not the boss."
9. **rifle** *n.* a long gun fired from the shoulder   "All of the soldiers have <u>rifles</u>."
10. **season** *n.* a time of the year for some activity, for example, a sport   "The football <u>season</u> begins in September."
11. **shoot** *v.* to send a bullet from a gun; to fire a gun   "Take my money and my watch, but don't <u>shoot</u>."
12. **woods** (plural) *n.* an area with many trees, but smaller than a forest   "Edna and I like to walk in the <u>woods</u>."

PREVIEW QUESTIONS

Discuss these questions before reading the dialog.

1. Do you think it's OK to hunt—to kill animals for sport? Explain your answer.
2. Did you ever go hunting? If so, where?

Ray is going hunting with his friend Mike. Ray loves the outdoors. But his friend Alicia doesn't believe in hunting.

Alicia: What are you doing with that rifle?

Ray: It's the hunting season. I'm going hunting with Mike.

Alicia: Why do you go hunting?

Ray: Mostly for the fresh air and exercise. I love the outdoors.

Alicia: Where do you go?

Ray: To the woods about ten miles from here.

Alicia: I don't believe in hunting.

Ray: Why not?

Alicia: I don't think we should kill animals.

Ray: But you eat beef.

Alicia: It's OK to kill animals for food, but not for fun.

Ray: There's more to hunting than fun. There are too many deer in the woods.

Alicia: But they're so beautiful. How can you kill them?

Ray: I don't think about it. I just shoot.

COMPREHENSION

Answer these questions about the dialog. Use your own ideas to answer questions with an asterisk.

1. What is Ray doing with a rifle?
2. Why does he go hunting?
3. Where does he go?
4. How does Alicia feel about hunting?
5. Why is she against hunting?
6. When does she think it's OK to kill animals?
*7. Do you think that Alicia's ideas will keep Ray from hunting? Explain your answer.

SHARING INFORMATION

Discuss these questions in pairs or small groups.

1. Do you have any friends or relatives who like to hunt?
2. Do you think it's OK to kill animals to make fur coats? Explain your answer.
3. Do you think we need more laws to control guns? Explain your answer.
4. Do you like outdoor activities? If so, name some that you like.

SENTENCE COMPLETION

Complete the sentences with these words.

woods	just	hunt	exercise	believe in

1. Stan plays tennis and basketball. He gets a lot of _____.
2. We like to watch the birds in the _____.
3. In many places in Africa, you're not allowed to _____ lions.
4. I don't _____ letting children watch a lot of TV.
5. _____ keep quiet and listen.

season	beef	shooting	outdoors	fun

6. Police officers have to be good at _____ a gun.
7. I like to play cards with my friends. It's _____.
8. Some countries have a rainy _____.
9. It's a beautiful day. We should spend some time _____.
10. I don't eat much _____.

A Hockey Star

1. **entirely** *adv.* completely; wholly "The house was <u>entirely</u> destroyed by fire."
2. **goal** *n.* a score in a soccer or hockey game "Our hockey team scored a <u>goal</u> with a minute to play, and we won the game 3 to 2."
3. **guess** *v.* or *n.* to think that something is probably true "I <u>guess</u> you like your new job."
4. **ice hockey** (often **hockey**) *n.* a sport played on ice, in which the players try to advance a puck and score (The *puck* is made of hard rubber and is round and flat.) "It's not easy to play <u>hockey</u>, but it's fun."
5. **mean** *v.* to wish to say "I don't know what this word <u>means</u>."
6. **news** *n.* new information "Did you hear the big <u>news</u>? Ted and Erin got engaged."
7. **next** *adj.* the one that comes after this one "My vacation begins <u>next</u> week."
8. **once** *adv.* one time "I take this medicine <u>once</u> a day."
9. **proud (of)** *adj.* to be very pleased with what one is or has "We're <u>proud of</u> our school."
10. **rough** *adj.* not gentle "Mr. Allen is <u>rough</u>. That's why I'm afraid of him."
11. **score** *v.* or *n.* to make points in a game "Danielle <u>scored</u> 20 points in the basketball game."
12. **silly** *adj.* foolish "I think it's <u>silly</u> to worry about the past."
13. **spirit** *n.* energy "Our team always tries hard. It has a lot of <u>spirit</u>."
14. **star** *n.* or *v.* a great player "Sammy Sosa is a baseball <u>star</u>."

PREVIEW QUESTIONS

Discuss these questions before reading the dialog.

1. Do you like ice hockey? Do you ever watch it on TV?
2. Today some girls play ice hockey. Do you think it is better for them to have their own teams, or is it better for them to play on the same teams as boys? Explain your answer.

Kathy is returning from a hockey game in which her daughter, Jennifer, scored three goals. Kathy is telling Betty, her mother, about the game.

Kathy: I have some great news, Mom!

Betty: What is it?

Kathy: Jennifer scored three goals in today's game.

Betty: What does that mean?

Kathy: Your granddaughter is a hockey star.

Betty: I'm glad to hear that, but . . .

Kathy: But what?

Betty: I don't think girls should play hockey. It's too rough.

Kathy: Don't be silly, Mom! A lot of girls play hockey today.

Betty: Yes, and some girls smoke. Does that make it right?

Kathy: Of course not, but smoking is entirely different.

Betty: I guess you're right.

Kathy: Why don't you come to Jenn's next game?

Betty: OK. I'll go just once.

Kathy: That's the spirit! You'll be proud of Jenn.

TRUE OR FALSE

If the sentence is true, write T. *If it's false, write* F.

_____ 1. Jennifer is a very good hockey player.

_____ 2. Betty thinks it's OK for girls to play hockey.

_____ 3. Kathy thinks hockey is too rough for girls.

_____ 4. Betty compares playing hockey and smoking.

_____ 5. Kathy invites her mom to the next hockey game.

_____ 6. Her mom won't go.

SHARING INFORMATION

Discuss these questions in pairs or small groups.

1. Why do you think hockey is so popular in Canada?
2. Do schools today give girls as many opportunities to play sports as they give boys? If not, why not?
3. Do you think the media (newspapers, magazines, TV) pays enough attention to women's sports? Explain your answer.
4. Betty says that some girls smoke. Why do some young people smoke when they know that smoking can cause cancer?

MATCHING

Match the words in Column A with their definitions or descriptions in Column B. Print the letters on the blank lines.

Column A	Column B
_____ 1. tired	A. a unit of weight
_____ 2. too	B. very pleased with
_____ 3. pound	C. clean and cool
_____ 4. beef	D. a great player
_____ 5. fresh	E. an area with many trees
_____ 6. rifle	F. needing rest
_____ 7. woods	G. the meat of a cow
_____ 8. proud (of)	H. the one after this
_____ 9. star	I. more than is good
_____ 10. next	J. a long gun

Roberto Clemente

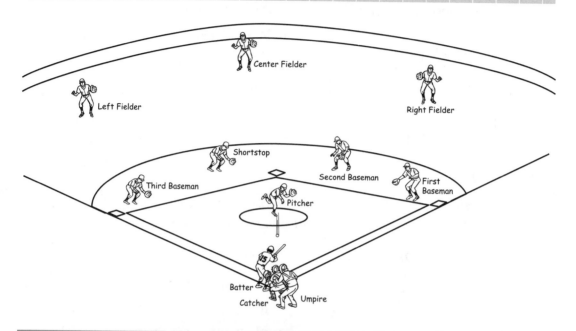

Center Fielder

Left Fielder

Right Fielder

Shortstop

Second Baseman

Third Baseman

First Baseman

Pitcher

Batter

Catcher

Umpire

WORD BANK

1. **against** *prep.* in opposition to "We're playing <u>against</u> a very good team today."
2. **be crazy about** *idiom* to love very much "Cindy sings and plays the piano. She <u>is crazy about</u> music."
3. **career** *n.* a job that requires education or special talent, for example, acting "Chen is going to law school to prepare for a <u>career</u> as a lawyer."
4. **contract** *n.* a formal agreement, usually in writing "The workers did not accept the <u>contract</u> that the company offered them. They want more money."
5. **kid** (informal) *n.* a child "Craig and Beth have two <u>kids</u>, a boy and a girl."
6. **perfect** *adj.* the best possible "We had <u>perfect</u> weather for our picnic."
7. **scout** *n.* or *v.* a person who looks for good players for a college or professional team "Two college <u>scouts</u> came to our high-school football game."
8. **sign** *v.* to write one's name on something, for example, a letter, a contract, a check "Kristina <u>signed</u> a check for $100."
9. **skinny** *adj.* very thin "I don't know why Carl is <u>skinny</u>. He eats a lot."
10. **sugar cane** *n.* a tropical plant from which we get sugar "They grow a lot of <u>sugar cane</u> in Cuba and the Dominican Republic."
11. **teammate** *n.* another player on the same team "Fran is talking to a <u>teammate</u>."
12. **throw** *n.* or *v.* the result of throwing (To *throw* is to send something through the air.) "The catcher made a good <u>throw</u> to second base."

PREVIEW QUESTIONS

Discuss these questions before reading the story.

1. Do you like baseball? Do you ever watch it on TV? Do or did you ever play it?
2. Roberto Clemente was from Puerto Rico. Where is Puerto Rico? Is it a large island?
3. Baseball is the number one sport in Puerto Rico and the Dominican Republic. Why do you think baseball is so popular in those lands?

The skinny kid made a perfect throw from center field to the catcher. Al Campanis, a scout for the Brooklyn Dodgers,[1] was watching. The kid's name was Roberto. He ran 40 yards in 4.6 seconds—very fast time. Then he hit well against a good pitcher, and that was enough for Campanis. The Dodgers signed Roberto to a $10,000 contract. He was only 19.

Roberto Clemente was born in Carolina, Puerto Rico, on August 18, 1934. He was the youngest of six children. His father worked in the sugar-cane fields and made four dollars a week. His mother washed clothes at night to help pay the bills.

Roberto was crazy about baseball, and he and his friends played for hours. In one game, he hit ten home runs.

After the Dodgers signed Roberto, they sent him to Montreal to play for their best minor-league[2] team. He had a difficult year. He missed his family and friends, and his mother's cooking. His teammates spoke English, but he knew very little English. After a year in Montreal, the Pittsburgh Pirates signed Roberto, and he played his entire major-league career for them.

1. The **Brooklyn Dodgers** were a major-league[2] baseball team. In 1958, they moved from Brooklyn to Los Angeles. Today they are the Los Angeles Dodgers.
2. Baseball has two **major leagues**, the National League and the American League. These leagues have the best baseball teams in the world. **Minor-league** teams are not as good.

COMPREHENSION

Answer these questions about the story. Use your own ideas to answer questions with an asterisk.

Paragraph 1

1. What did Roberto do that first made Campanis notice him?
2. What was Campanis?
3. How did he know that Roberto was very fast?
4. What did the Dodgers offer Roberto?

Paragraph 2

5. What did Roberto's father do?
*6. Did you think work in the sugar-cane fields is difficult? Explain your answer.
7. What did Roberto's mother do at night? Why?

Paragraph 3

8. How many home runs did Roberto hit in one game?

Paragraph 4

9. Why did Roberto have a difficult year in Montreal?
*10. The weather in Montreal was sometimes a problem for him. Why?
11. What major-league team signed him?
12. How long did he play for them?

SHARING INFORMATION

Discuss these questions in pairs or small groups.

1. Roberto Clemente was always a U.S. citizen. Why?
2. Name some countries, besides the United States, where baseball is very popular.
3. When Roberto started playing in Montreal, he knew very little English. Why did this make it harder for him to play?
4. Roberto got $10,000 for signing with the Dodgers. Was $10,000 worth a lot more in 1954 than today? Explain your answer.
5. What do you think he did with his $10,000?
6. Was Roberto Clemente a great baseball player mostly because of natural talent, or mostly because he played so much? Explain your answer.

STORY COMPLETION

Baseball and the Dominican Republic

Baseball is the number one sport in the Dominican Republic, and the country produces a lot of good players. Major-league teams offer some players money to go to their camps and to play in their summer league in the Dominican Republic.

kids	scouts	enough	crazy about
sign	entire	contracts	career

Baseball is the favorite sport in the Dominican Republic, and it seems that the _____ country is _____ the game. Many of the _____ there are very good players, and a baseball _____ is their big hope.

Major-league teams send _____ to the country, and they offer the better players _____ to go to their camps and to play in their summer league in the Dominican Republic.

The players may get four or five thousand dollars when they _____, but only a few of them are good _____ to play in the major leagues.

The Hall of Fame

ROBERTO WALKER CLEMENTE
PITTSBURGH N. L. 1955-1972

MEMBER OF EXCLUSIVE 3,000-HIT CLUB. LED
NATIONAL LEAGUE IN BATTING FOUR TIMES.
HAD FOUR SEASONS WITH 200 OR MORE HITS
WHILE POSTING LIFETIME .317 AVERAGE AND
240 HOME RUNS. WON MOST VALUABLE PLAYER
AWARD 1966. RIFLE-ARMED DEFENSIVE STAR
SET N.L. MARK BY PACING OUTFIELDERS IN
ASSISTS FIVE YEARS. BATTED .362 IN TWO
WORLD SERIES, HITTING IN ALL 14 GAMES.

Source: National Baseball Hall of Fame, Cooperstown, New York

WORD BANK

1. **cargo** *n.* the goods (things) carried by ship, plane, or truck "The <u>cargo</u> ship is bringing bananas to the United States."
2. **catch** *n.* or *v.* the act of catching (To *catch* is to stop a ball with your hands and hold it.) "Ricky made a very good <u>catch</u> in today's game."
3. **crash (into)** *v.* or *n.* to hit with great force "The bus <u>crashed into</u> a car."
4. **die** *v.* to stop living "Ruth is old and very sick. She may <u>die</u> soon."
5. **earthquake** *n.* a sudden moving of the ground that often causes a lot of damage "The <u>earthquake</u> destroyed many homes."
6. **elect** *v.* to choose by voting "Every four years we <u>elect</u> a President."
7. **hit (base hit)** *n.* the result of hitting a baseball where the other team can't catch it or throw it to first base before the hitter "Reggie got two <u>hits</u> in the big game."
8. **however** *conj.* but "I'm very busy. <u>However</u>, I can see you for a few minutes."
9. **off** *prep.* away from land "Dennis and Monica went fishing <u>off</u> the coast of Florida."
10. **retire** *v.* to stop using something "The bus company is <u>retiring</u> its old buses."
11. **supplies** (plural) *n.* the things we need to do something "Do we have enough <u>supplies</u> for our trip?"
12. **take off** *v.* or *n.* to go up into the air in a plane "The plane is going to <u>take off</u>."
13. **terrible** *adj.* very bad "Brad was in a <u>terrible</u> auto accident and is in the hospital."
14. **uniform** *n.* the clothing which all the members of a group wear, for example, soldiers and police officers "Our baseball team has new <u>uniforms</u>."
15. **valuable** *adj.* of great use or help (The *most valuable player* (**MVP**) is the player who most helped his or her team in a game or season.) "They named Debbie the most <u>valuable</u> player on her basketball team."

PREVIEW QUESTIONS

Discuss these questions before reading the story.

1. Roberto Clemente was a very fast runner. Why is it important that a baseball player, especially an outfielder, be fast?
2. Earthquakes are very dangerous. Were you ever in an earthquake? Was it a big one?
3. Baseball honors its greatest players in its Hall of Fame.[1] Did you ever hear of the Hall of Fame? Do you think it's a good idea?

Roberto Clemente was a great hitter. He won the National League batting title[2] four times, and in 1972 got his 3,000th major-league hit. He was only the 11th player in the history of baseball to get 3,000 hits.

Roberto was also a very good right fielder. He was very fast, made many great catches, and had a strong arm. In 1966, the sports writers voted Roberto the most valuable player (MVP) in the National League.

However, Roberto Clemente was much more than a baseball star. He liked to help people. When he heard about a terrible earthquake in Managua, Nicaragua, he offered to help. On December 31, 1972, he took off in an old cargo plane filled with food and supplies for the people of Managua. But the plane crashed into the sea a mile off the shore of Puerto Rico. Everyone on the plane died. The people of Puerto Rico and the Pittsburgh Pirates lost a great player and a great man.

On March 20, 1973, Roberto Clemente was elected to the Baseball Hall of Fame, an honor given to very few players. And on April 5, 1973, the Pittsburgh Pirates retired number 21—Clemente's uniform number. No player on the Pirates will ever wear that number again.

---

1. The **Baseball Hall of Fame** is located in Cooperstown, New York. It is a large building, and on its walls are plaques that honor the players elected to the Hall of Fame.
2. In sports, a person or team that is number one wins the *title*. "Our football team won the state title." The baseball player with the highest batting average wins the **batting title.**

COMPREHENSION

Answer these questions about the story. Use your own ideas to answer questions with an asterisk.

Paragraph 1

    1. How many batting titles did Roberto Clemente win?

    2. How many major-league hits did he get?

Paragraph 2

    3. What position did Roberto play?

 *4. Why does an outfielder need a strong arm?

    5. What honor did Roberto receive in 1966?

Paragraph 3

    6. Why was Roberto bringing food and supplies to Managua, Nicaragua?

    7. What happened to his plane?

Paragraph 4

    8. To what was Roberto elected on March 20, 1973?

    9. How did the Pirates honor him?

*10. Teams often retire the numbers of their great players. Do you think that is a good way to honor them? Explain your answer.

SHARING INFORMATION

Discuss these questions in pairs or small groups.

1. Baseball has the best-known Hall of Fame. Did you know that football, basketball, and hockey also have Halls of Fame? In what country do you think the Hockey Hall of Fame is?
2. What are some of the advantages of being a professional baseball player? And some of the disadvantages? (the advantages = the good things about; the disadvantages = the bad things about)
3. Do you think sports stars should use some of their time and money to help others as Roberto Clemente did? Do you think most of them do?
4. Today most major-league baseball players make more money than the President of the United States. Is that OK? Explain your answer.
5. Do you admire Roberto more because he was a very good baseball player, or because he was willing to put his life in danger to help those in need? Explain your answer.
6. Roberto Clemente was not afraid of flying. Are you?

SENTENCE COMPLETION

Complete the sentences with these words.

earthquakes	took off	cargo	however	terrible

1. We have 18 inches of snow. Driving is _____.
2. The army is using a _____ plane to send food to the soldiers.
3. In many places in California people worry about _____.
4. Evan is very smart. _____, he doesn't study much.
5. The plane to Chicago _____ 20 minutes ago.

supplies	elected	uniforms	valuable	dying

6. The flowers were pretty, but they're _____ now.
7. Our club _____ a new secretary.
8. That's a very _____ watch.
9. Put the pencils, paper, and other _____ in the cabinet.
10. In some countries, all school children wear _____.

TRUE OR FALSE

If the sentence is true, write T. *If it's false, write* F *and change it to a true statement.*

_____ 1. Many parents are proud of their kids.

_____ 2. There are a lot of trees in the woods.

_____ 3. Sitting in a chair is good exercise.

_____ 4. Football is a rough sport.

_____ 5. People are skinny because they eat a lot.

_____ 6. It's silly to work hard.

_____ 7. Scouts look for good players.

SYNONYMS

Synonyms are words that have the same or a similar meaning. Next to each sentence, write a synonym for the underlined word or words.

fun	silly	lucky	however
entire	kids	just	hurt

1. You're <u>fortunate</u> you have a good job. _____
2. Many people were <u>injured</u> in the earthquake. _____
3. Have <u>a good time</u> at the picnic. _____
4. I'm <u>only</u> trying to help you. _____
5. Did you read the <u>whole</u> book? _____
6. Justin asks a lot of <u>foolish</u> questions. _____
7. I ate a good breakfast. <u>But</u> I'm still hungry _____
8. The <u>children</u> are eating lunch. _____

ANTONYMS

Antonyms are words that have opposite meanings. In the blank spaces, write an antonym for each word.

rough	glad	die	terrible
against	major	skinny	off

1. live   _____
2. minor   _____
3. on   _____
4. gentle   _____
5. fat   _____
6. for   _____
7. unhappy   _____
8. very good _____

3

Celebrations

The Fourth of July

1. **band** *n.* a group of people that plays music, especially popular music "The <u>band</u> at the dance was very good."
2. **cookout** *n.* a meal cooked and eaten outdoors, often with hot dogs and hamburgers "We're having a <u>cookout</u> this Sunday. I hope you can come."
3. **fireworks** (plural) *n.* a public show in which explosives are used to produce light and noise "Many cities have <u>fireworks</u> on July 4."
4. **Independence Day** *n.* July 4, the day on which the United States declared its independence from England "<u>Independence Day</u> is a big holiday in the United States."
5. **join** *v.* to do something with others "Can you <u>join</u> us for dinner?"
6. **parade** *n.* or *v.* a celebration in which people march, usually with bands "Every Thanksgiving Day there is a big <u>parade</u> in New York City."
7. **pool (swimming pool)** *n.* a small area of water for swimming "We have a <u>pool</u> in our back yard."
8. **report** *n.* or *v.* a written or spoken statement, for example, about the weather "The police officer wrote a <u>report</u> about the accident."
9. **sunny** *adj.* with lots of sun "I hope we get a <u>sunny</u> day for our trip."
10. **swimsuit** *n.* what one wears when one swims "Lindsay is buying a <u>swimsuit</u>."

PREVIEW QUESTIONS

Discuss these questions before reading the dialog.

1. What are some of the ways in which people in the United States celebrate July 4, Independence Day?
2. Do you do anything special on July 4? If so, what?

Karen is talking to her cousin Gene. She's married and he's single. Karen is inviting him to a cookout on July 4.

Karen: Tomorrow is Independence Day.

Gene: I know. What's the weather report?

Karen: Hot and sunny. What are you doing tomorrow?

Gene: In the morning, I'm going to the parade.

Karen: We're having a cookout in the afternoon. Why don't you come?

Gene: Thanks, I will. I love cookouts.

Karen: Bring your swimsuit. We have a new pool.

Gene: Great!

Karen: And we're going to the park at night.

Gene: To watch the fireworks?

Karen: Yes, and to listen to the band.

Gene: Can I join you?

Karen: Sure. Why not?

COMPREHENSION

Answer these questions about the dialog. Use your own ideas to answer questions with an asterisk.

1. What is the weather report for July 4?
2. Where is Gene going in the morning?
3. What is Karen having in the afternoon?
4. Why does she want him to bring a swimsuit?
5. Why is she going to the park? Give two reasons.
6. Is Gene going with her?
*7. What kind of music do you think the band will play? Explain your answer.

SHARING INFORMATION

Discuss these questions in pairs or small groups.

1. Do you like to watch parades? Do you ever watch them on TV? If so, when?
2. Do you like cookouts? Explain your answer.
3. Do you watch fireworks on July 4? If so, where?
4. Does your country have an Independence Day? When is it? How is it celebrated?

DICTATION

1. *Listen while the teacher reads the dialog without stopping. Don't write anything.*

2. *The teacher will read the dialog a second time, pausing after the missing lines. Write in the missing lines.*

3. *The teacher will read the dialog a third time. Check your work.*

Gene: What's the weather report?

Karen: _____

Gene: In the morning, I'm going to the parade.

Karen: _____

Gene: Thanks, I will. I love cookouts.

Karen: _____

Gene: Great!

Karen: _____

Gene: To watch the fireworks?

Karen: _____

Trick or Treat

WORD BANK

1. **astronaut** *n.* a person who goes into outer space "Neil Armstrong was the first astronaut to walk on the moon."

2. **candle** *n.* a round piece of wax with a string in the middle which gives light when it burns "There are ten candles on Ryan's birthday cake."

3. **Halloween** *n.* a holiday on which children wear costumes and go from door to door asking people for candy or other small gifts "Halloween always comes on October 31."

4. **me too** *idiom* an informal way to say "I do too." or "I am too." "Shannon likes to swim." "Me too."

5. **pirate** *n.* a person who stops ships to steal from them "The pirates took all the gold that was on the ship."

6. **pumpkin** *n.* a large, round, orange fruit often used to make pie "I love pumpkin pie."

7. **treat** *n.* or *v.* something special we like to eat or do "Ice cream is my favorite treat."

8. **trick** *n.* or *v.* a joke "Some students like to play tricks on their teachers."

9. **trick or treat** *idiom* On Halloween, children go from house to house and ask for candy, saying *"Trick or treat."* This means give me a *treat*, or I will play a *trick* on you.

PREVIEW QUESTIONS

Discuss these questions before reading the dialog.

1. Halloween is a special holiday in which children have a lot of fun. Is there a special holiday for children in your country? If so, explain it.
2. Why do you think many adults also enjoy Halloween?

Tomorrow is Halloween. Janet is in the kitchen, putting a candle in a pumpkin. Matt is her husband. They have two children, Greg and Stephanie.

Matt:	Where are you?
Janet:	In the kitchen.
Matt:	What are you doing?
Janet:	I'm putting a candle in a pumpkin.
Matt:	Oh, that's right. Tomorrow is Halloween.
Janet:	I love Halloween.
Matt:	Me too. It's a lot of fun, especially for the kids.
Janet:	Greg is going to be a pirate.
Matt:	And Stephanie?
Janet:	An astronaut.
Matt:	What are we giving the kids who come to the door?
Janet:	Nickels.
Matt:	Good idea. They get too much candy.
Janet:	That's right. And some of them get sick from it.
Matt:	Besides, kids love money.
Janet:	Don't we all?

TRUE OR FALSE

If the sentence is true, write T. *If it's false, write* F.

_____   1. Janet is making a pumpkin pie.

_____   2. She doesn't like Halloween.

_____   3. Matt thinks Halloween is fun.

_____   4. Greg is going to be someone who is dangerous.

_____   5. Janet is going to give the kids money.

_____   6. Matt wants to give them candy.

SHARING INFORMATION

Discuss these questions in pairs or small groups.

1. Do you think kids are happier when they get candy, or when they get money? Explain your answer.
2. What do you like most about Halloween?
3. What do you (or your parents) give kids on Halloween?
4. Why should parents check the candy kids get on Halloween?

STORY COMPLETION

Bobby's Birthday

Bobby is going to be eight years old tomorrow. Twenty of his friends are coming to his party. His mother is buying soda and cake for the party.

Complete the story with these words.

a lot of	sick	fun	candles
especially	candy	too much	kids

Tomorrow is Bobby's birthday. He's going to be eight years old. He can't wait for his birthday and _____ for his party. Parties are always _____.

Twenty _____ are coming to the party. Bobby's mother is buying _____ soda and _____ for the party. She's also getting a cake and some _____ to put on it.

Last year Bobby ate _____ at his party and got _____. This year he's going to more careful about how much he eats.

Turkey Day

WORD BANK

1. **balloon** *n.* a small, thin rubber bag that we fill with air or other gas "I'm going to buy some <u>balloons</u> for the dance."
2. **celebrate** *v.* to do something special on a holiday or birthday, for example, have a party "How are you going to <u>celebrate</u> New Year's Day?"
3. **excited** *adj.* having strong feelings "Omar is <u>excited</u> about his new job."
4. **last** *adj.* coming after all the others; final "The students are happy because it is the <u>last</u> day of school."
5. **Macy's** *n.* a large department store that runs a big parade in New York City on Thanksgiving morning "I like to shop at <u>Macy's</u>."
6. **mashed potatoes** *n.* potatoes that are boiled in water and pressed down (A little milk and butter are usually added to the potatoes.) "We're having steak and <u>mashed potatoes</u> for dinner."
7. **together** *adv.* with one another; in a group "Ed and Jay often study <u>together</u>."
8. **turkey** *n.* a large bird that many people have for dinner on Thanksgiving "We always have <u>turkey</u> on Thanksgiving."
9. **wonderful** *adj.* very good "Kate is a <u>wonderful</u> cook."

PREVIEW QUESTIONS

Discuss these questions before reading the dialog.

1. Some cities have parades on Thanksgiving Day. Did you ever go to a Thanksgiving parade or watch one on TV?
2. Do people in your country eat much turkey?

Yoko and her friend Sue are talking about their plans for Thanksgiving. Yoko is going to the parade in New York City, and Sue is going to a high-school football game.

Yoko: Thanksgiving is a wonderful holiday!

Sue: Yes, it brings families together.

Yoko: And everyone celebrates it.

Sue: Are you doing anything special for Thanksgiving?

Yoko: We're taking the kids to the Macy's parade in New York City.

Sue: They must be excited.

Yoko: Very. They love the big balloons.

Sue: We're going to the high-school football game.

Yoko: Of course. Your son plays on the team.

Sue: That's right. And it's the last game of the season.

Yoko: I hope you win.

Sue: Thanks. What are you having for Thanksgiving dinner?

Yoko: Turkey, mashed potatoes, and pumpkin pie.

Sue: That's exactly what we're having. Happy Thanksgiving!

Yoko: You too.

COMPREHENSION

Answer these questions about the dialog. Use your own ideas to answer questions with an asterisk.

1. Where is Yoko taking the kids on Thanksgiving?
2. How do the kids feel about going to the parade?
3. What do they love to see at the parade?
4. Where is Sue going on Thanksgiving?
5. Why is she going?
6. What is Yoko having for Thanksgiving dinner? And Sue?
*7. Macy's Thanksgiving parade is especially for kids. Do you think adults also enjoy the parade? Explain your answer.

SHARING INFORMATION

Discuss these questions in pairs or small groups.

1. What is your favorite holiday? Why?
2. What do you usually do on Thanksgiving?
3. Do you usually have turkey on Thanksgiving? If not, what do you have?
4. Tell about a holiday you celebrate in your country that we don't celebrate in the United States.

SENTENCE COMPLETION

Complete the sentences with these words.

excited	wonderful	together	last	balloon

1. The play was _____. I loved it.
2. By the _____ period, most of the students and teachers are tired.
3. Leonid gets _____ when he watches soccer games on TV.
4. I'm getting Paula a big _____ for her birthday.
5. My cousin and I like to go to the movies _____.

season	win	hope	special	team

6. We have a very good volleyball _____ this year.

7. It should _____ most of its games.

8. I want you to meet Fred. He's a _____ friend of mine.

9. The major-league baseball _____ begins in April.

10. I _____ you can come to our party.

Birthday Presents

WORD BANK

1. **borrow** *v.* to take or receive something that you have to return "Sid let me <u>borrow</u> his car to go to the doctor."
2. **earring** *n.* jewelry for one's ears "Judy's <u>earrings</u> are very pretty."
3. **fantastic** *adj.* great; very good "You'll love this restaurant. The food is <u>fantastic</u>."
4. **last** *v.* to stay in good condition "These are good shoes. They'll <u>last</u> a long time."
5. **mind** *v.* to be unhappy about; to dislike (used especially in questions and negative statements) "You can use my phone. I don't <u>mind</u>."
6. **once in a while** *idiom* not very often; sometimes "Gina goes to the movies <u>once in a while</u>."
7. **pair** *n.* two things that are the same and that are used together, for example, a *pair* of socks "I need a new <u>pair</u> of gloves."
8. **portable** *adj.* easy to carry or move "Don is bringing his <u>portable</u> TV to the beach."
9. **suggest** *v.* to say that something is a good idea "My English teacher <u>suggested</u> that I read more."
10. **yet** *adv.* up to now; now (used in questions and negative statements) "We didn't eat <u>yet</u>."

PREVIEW QUESTIONS

Discuss these questions before reading the dialog.

1. In the United States, birthdays are celebrated with gifts, parties, and cakes. How are birthdays celebrated in your country? Are there any differences?
2. What are some common birthday presents parents give their children?

Linda is talking to her brother, Darryl, about getting presents for each of their children. Both children have birthdays in July. He's buying a bike for his son, Jason; she doesn't know yet what to get her daughter, Michelle.

Linda: What are you getting Jason for his birthday?
Darryl: A new bike.
Linda: That's nice. How much will it cost?
Darryl: About $130.
Linda: That's not bad, and it'll last for years.
Darryl: What are you getting Michelle?
Linda: I don't know yet. What do you suggest?
Darryl: A pair of earrings.
Linda: No, her grandmother is getting her earrings.
Darryl: How about a portable CD player?
Linda: Fantastic. She loves music.
Darryl: And you can borrow it once in a while.
Linda: That's right. She won't mind.

TRUE OR FALSE

If the sentence is true, write T. *If it's false, write* F.

_____ 1. Jason's bike will cost about $130.

_____ 2. Linda thinks that's too much money.

_____ 3. Darryl suggests earrings as a gift for Michelle.

_____ 4. Linda is going to get her a portable radio.

_____ 5. Michelle likes to listen to music.

_____ 6. She'll be unhappy if her mother uses her CD player.

SHARING INFORMATION

Discuss these questions in pairs or small groups.

1. Do you ever ride a bike? Do you ride a lot?
2. Do you like to listen to CDs?
3. Does listening to them help you to learn English? Does it help a lot?
4. Name some things people borrow.

MATCHING

Match the words in Column A with their definitions or descriptions in Column B. Print the letters on the blank lines.

	Column A	Column B
_____	1. astronaut	A. it gives light
_____	2. turkey	B. a large, orange fruit
_____	3. pool	C. a person who steals from ships
_____	4. candle	D. two that are the same
_____	5. pirate	E. a large bird
_____	6. report	F. up to now
_____	7. pumpkin	G. a small area of water for swimming
_____	8. band	H. a person who goes into outer space
_____	9. yet	I. a written or spoken statement
_____	10. pair	J. a group that plays music

The Pilgrims

WORD BANK

1. **decide** *v.* to consider and to choose "We <u>decided</u> to go to Canada for one week."
2. **get** *v.* to become "I'm <u>getting</u> hungry."
3. **go back** *v.* to return "Carlos is <u>going back</u> to Colombia to live."
4. **God** *n.* the creator and ruler of the world "The Pilgrims thanked <u>God</u> and asked for His help."
5. **grateful** *adj.* feeling or expressing thanks "Laura helped me get a job, and I'm very <u>grateful</u>."
6. **head** *v.* or *n.* to go in a certain direction "The train is <u>heading</u> to Chicago."
7. **land** *v.* or *n.* to come to shore; to bring a plane to the ground "The ship <u>landed</u> in Boston." "The plane <u>landed</u> at Kennedy Airport."
8. **own** *adj.* or *v.* having for oneself "Dorothy has her <u>own</u> car."
9. **Pilgrims** *n.* a religious group from England who came to America in 1620 because the King of England did not allow them to worship freely "The <u>Pilgrims</u> came to America on the Mayflower."
10. **plant** *v.* or *n.* to put seeds in the ground "Larry is <u>planting</u> flowers in his garden."
11. **sail** *v.* or *n.* to travel by ship "The ship is <u>sailing</u> from New York to France."
12. **ship** *n.* or *v.* a large boat "The <u>ship</u> is crossing the Pacific Ocean."
13. **show how** *v.* to teach someone, especially by example "Sandra <u>showed</u> me <u>how</u> to play the piano."
14. **worship** *v.* or *n.* to honor and love, especially God "People <u>worship</u> God in churches, synagogues, and mosques."

PREVIEW QUESTIONS

Discuss these questions before reading the story.

1. In 1620, the Pilgrims came to America by ship. How did you come?
2. It took the Pilgrims 76 days to get to America from England. How long did it take you to get here from your country?
3. The Pilgrims arrived at Plymouth in December, the beginning of winter. Why was that a problem?

    On September 16, 1620, a ship sailed from England and headed to America. The name of the ship was the Mayflower. There were 102 men, women, and children on the ship, and many of them were Pilgrims.

The Pilgrims wanted to worship God in their own way, but the King of England didn't allow that. They decided to go to America to worship God as they wished.

On December 21, 1620, the Pilgrims landed at Plymouth, Massachusetts. It was the beginning of winter, and they didn't have enough food. Many got sick and died, but the Pilgrims didn't want to go back to England.

Friendly Native Americans[1] helped the Pilgrims. They showed them how to fish and how to plant corn and other vegetables.

By the fall of 1621, the Pilgrims had a lot of food. They were happy and grateful. They decided to have a parade and a big dinner to thank God and their Native American friends. They had turkey, fish, corn, and pumpkin. They invited many Native Americans to the dinner. After dinner, the Pilgrims and the Native Americans played games. This was the first Thanksgiving Day.

---

1. The **Native Americans** were the people who lived in America before the Europeans came. Columbus called them Indians because he thought he was in the Indies. Many Native Americans still live in different parts of the United States.

COMPREHENSION

*Answer these questions about the story. Use your own ideas to answer
questions with an asterisk.*

Paragraph 1

1. What was the name of the ship that sailed to America?
2. How many men, women, and children were on the ship?

Paragraph 2

3. What did the Pilgrims want?
4. Why couldn't they worship freely in England?

Paragraph 3

5. In what season did the Pilgrims land?
*6. They didn't want to go back to England. Do you think they also missed England? Explain your answer.

Paragraph 4

7. What did the Native Americans show the Pilgrims how to do? Name two things.
*8. Why was it important that the Pilgrims learn how to fish?

Paragraph 5

9. Why did the Pilgrims have a parade and a big dinner?
10. What did they have for dinner?

SHARING INFORMATION

Discuss these questions in pairs or small groups.

1. The Pilgrims came to America with their children. Why did this make it easier for the Native Americans to trust and accept the Pilgrims?
2. The Pilgrims and the Native Americans played games as part of their celebration of Thanksgiving. Which group was probably faster and stronger? Explain your answer.
3. Today a number of Native Americans still live near Plymouth. Some of them come to Plymouth on Thanksgiving Day to express their sorrow. Why?
4. The Pilgrims came to America to be free. Do you know of any group of immigrants who came to the United States to be free?
5. Name some things you are grateful for.
6. Who are you grateful to?

STORY COMPLETION

A Caribbean Vacation

Marty went on a vacation on a ship that stops at several Caribbean Islands. The first of them was Puerto Rico. Marty spent the morning in old San Juan and the afternoon at the beach.

Complete the story with these words.

sails	**landed**	**back**	**headed**
ship	**decided**	**own**	**winter**

Last _____, Marty _____ to take a vacation on a ship that _____ from Miami, Florida and stops at several Caribbean islands. He was traveling alone and had his _____ cabin.

The ship left Miami on Monday and _____ southeast. Early Tuesday morning, it _____ at San Juan, Puerto Rico.

In the morning, Marty visited Old San Juan, and in the afternoon he went swimming at a beautiful beach. Then he went _____ to the _____ for dinner. He had a wonderful day.

A Soldier

1. **courage** *n.* the quality that makes a person able to face danger and difficulties "Police officers need courage."
2. **kind** *adj.* friendly; ready to help "It's easy to work with Brett. He's so kind."
3. **pleased** *adj.* happy "I'm pleased with my new job."
4. **protect** *v.* to keep safe; to defend "Parents try to protect their children."
5. **stay** *v.* or *n.* to remain where one is "Henry is going to stay home today. He's sick."
6. **trust** *n.* or *v.* a feeling that someone is honest and wants to help "I know Alexandra well. We can put our trust in her."

PREVIEW QUESTIONS

Discuss these questions before reading the dialog.

1. The Pilgrims were a religious group that wanted peace, but they hired a soldier to come with them. Why?
2. Why do you think that all of the Pilgrims stayed in Plymouth when the Mayflower returned to England?

Squanto was one of the Native Americans who helped the Pilgrims. He knew English. He is talking to Miles Standish, a soldier who came to Plymouth with the Pilgrims.

Miles:	Hello, I'm Miles Standish.
Squanto:	Pleased to meet you, Miles. My name is Squanto.
Miles:	Nice to meet you Squanto. Come in and sit down.
Squanto:	Thanks. I'm teaching the Pilgrims how to plant corn.
Miles:	That's great! We need all the food we can get.
Squanto:	Are you a Pilgrim?
Miles:	No, but I work for them. They hired me.
Squanto:	To do what?
Miles:	To protect them. I'm a soldier.
Squanto:	I hear the Mayflower is returning to England.
Miles:	Yes, it is. Tomorrow morning.
Squanto:	Are any of the Pilgrims going back?
Miles:	No. They're all staying.
Squanto:	They have great courage.
Miles:	And great trust in God.
Squanto:	Is your family in Plymouth?
Miles:	My wife, Rose, was, but she died.
Squanto:	I'm sorry to hear that.
Miles:	Why don't you join me for dinner?
Squanto:	Thanks, that's very kind of you. I think I will.

COMPREHENSION

Answer these questions about the dialog. Use your own ideas to answer questions with an asterisk.

1. How did Squanto help the Pilgrims?
2. Why was it important for them to learn how to plant corn?
3. Who hired Miles?
4. What was his job?
5. What did Squanto hear?
6. When was the Mayflower returning?
7. None of the Pilgrims returned to England. What did that show? Name two things.
8. What was the name of Miles' wife? What happened to her?
9. What did Miles invite Squanto to do?
*10. Why do you think Squanto was happy to have dinner with Miles?

SHARING INFORMATION

Discuss these questions in pairs or small groups.

1. The Native Americans and Pilgrims were friends, but other Europeans and Native Americans were often enemies. Why?
2. Were the Europeans fair to the Native Americans? Explain your answer.
3. Do you think the Pilgrims were afraid of the Native Americans? Explain your answer.
4. Were the Native Americans afraid of the Pilgrims? Explain your answer.
5. Why was it much more dangerous to cross the ocean in 1620 than today?
6. The Pilgrims had great courage. Does it still take great courage to come from other countries to live in the United States? Explain your answer.
7. Miles Standish was a soldier. Do you think he also hunted when he lived in Plymouth? Explain your answer.

SENTENCE COMPLETION

Complete the sentences with these words.

pleased	kind	courage	protect	joined

1. Amy and I were going for a walk, and Marissa _____ us.
2. Colin is a good soldier. He has a lot of _____.
3. Shirley got 90 on her science test. She's _____.
4. In the summer, I wear sunglasses to _____ my eyes.
5. Most of the nurses are _____.

trust	died	planting	hiring	stay

6. Gabe is _____ tomatoes in his yard.
7. _____ here until I come back.
8. Denise is a very good doctor. You can put your _____ in her.
9. The high school is _____ three new teachers.
10. Derek is very sad. His dog _____.

TRUE OR FALSE

If the sentence is true, write T. *If it's false, write* F *and change it to a true statement.*

_____ 1. Bands often play in parades.

_____ 2. Astronauts don't need courage.

_____ 3. Pirates are very kind.

_____ 4. Many people eat hot dogs at cookouts.

_____ 5. Farmers plant candles in the spring.

_____ 6. We should be grateful to those who help us.

_____ 7. Teams celebrate when they win big games.

SYNONYMS

Synonyms are words that have the same or a similar meaning. Next to each sentence, write a synonym for the underlined word or words.

protect	portable	head	present
get	fantastic	pleased	last

1. Ali is <u>happy</u> with his new car. _____
2. The job of soldiers is to <u>defend</u> their country. _____
3. I'm going to buy a <u>gift</u> for Mary Ellen. _____
4. Don't <u>become</u> angry. _____
5. It's time to <u>go</u> home. _____
6. Jackie Robinson was a <u>great</u> baseball player. _____
7. The <u>final</u> chapter of the book is the best. _____
8. Is the radio <u>easy to carry</u>? _____

ANTONYMS

Antonyms are words that have opposite meanings. In the blank spaces, write an antonym for each word.

stay	friend	winter	together
give	sick	excited	win

1. summer _____
2. lose _____
3. leave _____
4. healthy _____
5. separately _____
6. enemy _____
7. calm _____
8. take _____

4

Love

The Big Dance

1. **angry** *adj.* feeling anger (*Anger* is a strong feeling we get when someone offends or disturbs us.) "I got very <u>angry</u> when Joan said I was stupid."
2. **answer** *v. or n.* to pick up a phone when it rings and speak to the person who is calling "The secretary always <u>answers</u> the phone."
3. **believe** *v.* to think that something is true "Dawn says she studied three hours for the test, and I <u>believe</u> her."
4. **better off** *idiom* in a better condition "Ron would be <u>better off</u> if he stopped drinking."
5. **calm down** *v.* to become less upset or excited; to become calm "<u>Calm down</u> and tell me what happened."
6. **fair** *adj.* what is right; just "Our teacher helps some students much more than others. That's not <u>fair</u>."
7. **jealous** *adj.* afraid of losing someone's love to another person "Harry gets <u>jealous</u> when he sees his girlfriend talking to other men."
8. **well** *idiom* a word used to introduce a statement "<u>Well</u>, I think you're wrong."

PREVIEW QUESTIONS

Discuss these questions before reading the dialog.

1. Dick is single and has two girlfriends. Is that OK? Explain your answer.
2. Do you think it's common to be jealous? Give an example of something that makes people jealous.

Dick has two girlfriends, Megan and Gloria. He invites Gloria to the big dance. Megan is upset and very angry. She's talking to her brother, Adam.

Adam: Why are you crying?

Megan: Dick didn't invite me to the big dance.

Adam: Why not?

Megan: He's going with Gloria.

Adam: I can't believe it.

Megan: Well, it's true. He must like her more than me.

Adam: Then you're better off without him.

Megan: I'm so angry and jealous. I'll never trust a man again.

Adam: Calm down! Take it easy! There are a lot of men in the world.

Megan: I can't calm down. It's not fair. I hate him.

Adam: Answer the phone. It's probably for you.

Megan: Hi, Ken. Yes, of course I will!

Adam: I bet Ken invited you to the dance.

Megan: He sure did. And he's much nicer than Dick. I'm so happy.

COMPREHENSION

Answer these questions about the dialog. Use your own ideas to answer questions with an asterisk.

1. Why is Megan crying?
2. Why didn't Dick invite her to the dance?
3. How does Megan feel about his inviting Gloria to the dance?
4. What does Megan say about men?
5. What advice does Adam give her?
6. What does Ken do?
*7. Do you think Dick will be surprised to see Megan at the dance? Explain your answer.

SHARING INFORMATION

Discuss these questions in pairs or small groups.

1. Do you think that women cry more than men? If so, why?
2. Who do you trust? Why?
3. Do you get jealous sometimes? Often? What makes you jealous?
4. Do you think young children get jealous easily? What makes them jealous?

DICTATION

1. *Listen while the teacher reads the dialog without stopping.* <u>*Don't write anything*</u>.

2. *The teacher will read the dialog a second time, pausing after the missing lines.* <u>*Write in the missing lines*</u>.

3. *The teacher will read the dialog a third time.* <u>*Check your work*</u>.

Adam: Why are you crying?

Megan: _____

Adam: Why not?

Megan: _____

Adam: I can't believe it.

Megan: _____

Adam: Then you're better off without him.

Megan: _____

Adam: Calm down! Take it easy! There are a lot of men in the world.

Megan: _____

The Matchmaker

WORD BANK

1. **attractive** *adj.* good-looking; pretty "Alima is an <u>attractive</u> girl and very nice."
2. **by the way** *idiom* also (We use *by the way* to introduce a new idea.) "<u>By the way</u>, did you know that Lynn and Gino are going to get married?"
3. **choice** *n.* the act of choosing; a person or thing one chooses (To *choose* is to select, to pick one thing from two or more.) "Ivan was my <u>choice</u> for class president."
4. **gain** *v.* or *n.* to obtain something useful "You will <u>gain</u> a lot by going to college."
5. **just** *adv.* a very short time ago "Aaron <u>just</u> left for work."
6. **match** *v.* or *n.* to arrange for a couple to meet and go out together "Peggy is trying to <u>match</u> me with her sister."
7. **matchmaker** *n.* a person who arranges for a couple to meet and go out together "Gladys is trying to find the perfect girl for Nathan. She's a good <u>matchmaker</u>."
8. **millionaire** *n.* a person who has a million dollars or more "Caroline is the president of a large company and a <u>millionaire</u>."
9. **real estate** *n.* land, houses, and buildings "<u>Real estate</u> in this neighborhood is very expensive."
10. **type** *n.* kind; a group of people or things that are similar "You know Adrian. What <u>type</u> of person is he?"

PREVIEW QUESTIONS

Discuss these questions before reading the dialog.

1. Where do most people meet the person they marry? At school? At work?
   Through a friend?
2. What do you think is the best age for a man to marry? And a woman?

Allison and Kevin are cousins. She's married, but Kevin is 30 and still single. He works for a real-estate agency.

Allison: Hi, Kevin. How's the real-estate business?

Kevin: Great! I just sold a house.

Allison: You're going to be a millionaire some day.

Kevin: Not by selling houses, I won't.

Allison: By the way, I want you to meet a friend of mine.

Kevin: Are you still trying to match me up with someone?

Allison: Sure. What's wrong with that?

Kevin: Nothing. Is she rich?

Allison: No, but she's attractive and very smart.

Kevin: OK, I have nothing to lose.

Allison: And a lot to gain. You'll like her.

Kevin: How do you know that?

Allison: I can tell. She's your type.

Kevin: Maybe, but what about your last choice? She certainly wasn't.

Allison: I know, but this one is different.

TRUE OR FALSE

If the sentence is true, write T. *If it's false, write* F.

_____ 1. Kevin plans to become a millionaire by selling houses.

_____ 2. Allison wants him to get married.

_____ 3. The woman he's going to meet is rich.

_____ 4. She is pretty and intelligent.

_____ 5. Kevin liked Allison's last choice.

_____ 6. Allison says the woman he's going to meet is different.

SHARING INFORMATION

Discuss these questions in pairs or small groups.

1. Do you think selling real estate is a good business? Explain your answer.
2. Does it require a lot of time and effort? Explain your answer.
3. Do you think you're going to be rich some day? If so, how?
4. How important is it (or was it) that the person you marry be good-looking? Explain your answer.

STORY COMPLETION

Buying a House

I was living in a house that was in poor condition. Fortunately, I was able to sell it with the help of a friend of mine and buy a much nicer one.

Complete the story with these words.

gain	**real-estate**	**choice**	**type**
attractive	**millionaire**	**still**	**sold**

The house I was living in was in poor condition, so I _____ it with the help of a _____ agent who went to school with me. We're _____ good friends.

My friend also helped me find and buy a small but _____ house in a quiet neighborhood with lots of trees. It was exactly the _____ of house I was looking for.

There was a larger house for sale on the same block, but it cost a lot more, and I'm not a _____, so it wasn't a difficult _____. Besides, I live alone and hate to clean. I have nothing to _____ by buying a large house.

A Lot in Common

WORD BANK

1. **argue** *v.* to fight with words   "Sal is a good friend of mine, but we often <u>argue</u> about sports and politics."
2. **bossy** *adj.* frequently telling others what to do; acting like a boss   "My older sister is <u>bossy</u>. She's always telling me to do this and to do that."
3. **compromise** *v.* or *n.* to disagree and then come to an agreement by having both sides get part of what they want   "My wife wanted to go to dinner at 6:00, and I wanted to go at 7:00. We <u>compromised</u> and went at 6:30."
4. **have in common** *idiom* to share the same interests and experiences   "Nicole and Brent <u>have</u> a lot <u>in common</u>. They went to the same school, and they love music and movies."
5. **just** *adv.* exactly   "Jeff looks <u>just</u> like his father."
6. **so** *adv.* also; too   "Lisa is a good student, and <u>so</u> is her brother."
7. **so** *adv.* used in place of repeating words from a previous sentence   "Is Drew coming to the party?" "I think <u>so</u>." (*So* is used in place of repeating *he is coming to the party.*)
8. **willing** *adj.* ready and happy to do something   "I'm <u>willing</u> to go shopping with you."

PREVIEW QUESTIONS

Discuss these questions before reading the dialog.

1. Do you think that most married couples have a lot in common?
2. How important is it to a happy marriage that a couple have a lot in common? Explain your answer.

    Anna is talking to her brother, Boris. He's in love with Nadia and wants to marry her, but there's a problem.

Anna: You look great today.

Boris: That's because I'm in love.

Anna: Who's the lucky girl?

Boris: Her name is Nadia.   I met her six months ago.

Anna: Are you thinking of getting married?

Boris: Yes, we have a lot in common, and she loves me, but there's a problem.

Anna: What is it?

Boris: She likes to argue, and she's bossy.

Anna: Just like you.

Boris: Exactly, and that's the problem.

Anna: Are you willing to compromise?

Boris: Yes, and so is she.

Anna: Then don't worry. You'll be happy.

Boris: I hope so.

COMPREHENSION

Answer these questions about the dialog. Use your own ideas to answer questions with an asterisk.

1. Why does Boris look great?
2. When did he meet Nadia?
3. Why does he want to marry her?
4. What problem do they have?
5. What are Boris and Nadia willing to do?
6. What advice does Anna give him?
*7. Do you think Boris and Nadia will be happy? Explain your answer.

SHARING INFORMATION

Discuss these questions in pairs or small groups.

1. What do you have in common with your spouse or best friend?
2. Do you like to argue? If so, about what?
3. Do you know anyone who is bossy?   Are you bossy?
4. Is it important that married couples be willing to compromise? Explain your answer.

SENTENCE COMPLETION

Complete the sentences with these words.

ago	in common	lucky	argues	so

1. I never get sick. I'm _____.
2. Mohammed came to the United States six months _____.
3. Is Keith going to the concert with us? I think _____.
4. I know Leslie, but we don't have much _____.
5. Corey is quiet and friendly. He almost never _____.

just	compromised	so	willing	bossy

6. I like Carmen, but she can be _____.
7. The children are tired, and _____ am I.
8. The baby looks _____ like her sister.
9. We're _____ to help you.
10. The company offered the workers $12 an hour, but they wanted $16. Both sides _____, and the workers are getting $14 an hour.

Valentine's Day

WORD BANK

1. **age** *n.* or *v.* how old a person or thing is "Some people don't want others to know their <u>age</u>."
2. **dozen** *adj.* twelve "I'm bringing soda and a <u>dozen</u> donuts to the picnic."
3. **engagement** *n.* a formal promise to marry someone "Alan and Sonia are having an <u>engagement</u> party this Friday."
4. **gee** *idiom* a very informal word expressing surprise "<u>Gee</u>, I didn't know that Chang was the president of the company."
5. **matter** *v.* to be important "You can sit any place you wish. It doesn't <u>matter</u>."
6. **old-fashioned** *adj.* thinking and acting as people did in the past "My uncle is only 40, but he's <u>old-fashioned</u>."
7. **secret** *n.* information we don't want others to know "Angie wouldn't tell us where she was going. She said it was a <u>secret</u>."
8. **So?** *idiom* Who cares?; that's not important "My father knows the mayor." "<u>So</u>? A lot of people know the mayor."
9. **Valentine's Day** *n.* On Saint <u>Valentine's Day</u> (February 14), we celebrate romantic love. Couples often give each other cards and go out to dinner. "Don't forget to get your wife something for <u>Valentine's Day</u>."

PREVIEW QUESTIONS

Discuss these questions before reading the dialog.

1. Do they celebrate Valentine's Day in your country? If so, do they celebrate it in the same way as in the United States?
2. If they don't celebrate Valentine's Day, is there another day on which people celebrate love? If so, tell us about it.

Joyce is talking to her cousin Steve. He's in love with Jessica. Tomorrow is Valentine's Day, and Steve is going to make it very special.

Joyce: Tomorrow is Valentine's Day.

Steve: I know, I'm taking Jessica to our favorite restaurant.

Joyce: Are you getting her flowers?

Steve: Yes, a dozen red roses and a very special gift.

Joyce: What is it?

Steve: Can you keep a secret?

Joyce: For one day, why not?

Steve: I'm giving Jessica an engagement ring.

Joyce: Congratulations! That's wonderful, but . . .

Steve: But what?

Joyce: Well, she's 32 and you're only 24.

Steve: But we're in love. Age doesn't matter.

Joyce: Maybe not, but the man is usually older.

Steve: So? Gee, you *are* old-fashioned.

Joyce: I guess I am.

TRUE OR FALSE

If the sentence is true, write T. *If it's false, write* F.

_____ 1. Steve is taking Jessica to the movies.

_____ 2. He is getting her 12 red roses.

_____ 3. Joyce says she can't keep a secret.

_____ 4. Steve wants to marry Jessica.

_____ 5. He is older than Jessica.

_____ 6. He says that age is not important if a couple is in love.

SHARING INFORMATION

Discuss these questions in pairs or small groups.

1. Do you have a favorite restaurant? If so, what's its name?
2. Are you good at keeping secrets?
3. When two adults are in love and want to marry, does age ever matter? Explain your answer.
4. Do you know anyone you consider old-fashioned? Who? Why do you consider the person old-fashioned?

MATCHING

Match the words in Column A with their definitions or descriptions in Column B. Print the letters on the blank lines.

Column A	Column B
_____ 1. believe	A. to arrange for a couple to meet
_____ 2. real estate	B. that's not important
_____ 3. bossy	C. ready and happy to do something
_____ 4. match	D. to think something is true
_____ 5. gee	E. frequently giving orders
_____ 6. secret	F. to fight with words
_____ 7. willing	G. a formal promise to marry
_____ 8. argue	H. something one doesn't want others to know
_____ 9. So?	I. land and buildings
_____ 10. engagement	J. expresses surprise

Hard at First

WORD BANK

1. **at first** *idiom* in the beginning   "<u>At first</u>, I didn't like Jonathan, but now we're good friends."
2. **dream** *n.* or *v.* something a person wants very much   "Stacey's <u>dream</u> is to be a doctor."
3. **get used to** *idiom* to get in the habit of   "Students have to <u>get used to</u> taking tests."
4. **lonely** *adj.* unhappy because one feels alone or misses friends   "Jane's husband went to Los Angeles on business. She's <u>lonely</u>."
5. **mix** *v.* to be with and talk to other people, for example, at a party   "The boss likes to <u>mix</u> with the workers."
6. **noisy** *adj.* making a lot of noise (*Noise* is a sound, especially an unpleasant one.)   "The restaurant is <u>noisy</u>."
7. **opportunity** *n.* an occasion a person has to do something good   "Mario has the <u>opportunity</u> to go to Europe this summer. I hope he goes."
8. **such** *adv.* very   "Mr. Robinson is <u>such</u> a nice person."

PREVIEW QUESTIONS

Discuss these questions before reading the story.

1. Some people come to the United States to get better jobs. Others come to study, or because their parents bring them. Why did you come?
2. In general, are schools in your country larger or smaller than those in the United States?
3. How are schools in your country different from those in the United States?

Joana came to the United States from Poland with her mother, father, and younger brother when she was 14. Her parents came because they wanted better jobs for themselves and more opportunities for their children.

At first, Joana's parents worked in a factory because they didn't know English. They didn't mind because they knew their children would have much better jobs.

The high school Joana attended was large, and only a few of the students were Polish. She didn't have any friends. Joana was lonely, didn't understand English, and wasn't used to such a big school. In Poland, she went to school with 400 students; in the United States she went with 2,400.

However, Joana was a good student, and most of the teachers were understanding. It wasn't long before she made friends and learned English. She also got used to the noisy lunch room, and mixing with students from many parts of the world.

Today Joana speaks perfect English, is a college graduate, and has a good job at the Valley National Bank. But her big dream is to become a lawyer, and she is going to law school at night.

COMPREHENSION

Answer these questions about the story. Use your own ideas to answer questions with an asterisk.

Paragraph 1
1. How old was Joana when she came to the United States?
2. Why did her parents come to the United States?

Paragraph 2
3. Where did Joana's parents work when they first came to the United States?
4. Why didn't they mind working in a factory?

Paragraph 3
5. Why was school difficult for Joana? Give three or four reasons.
*6. Was school (or work) difficult for you when you first came to the United States? Explain your answer.

Paragraph 4
7. What did Joana get used to in school?
*8. Do you think it was harder for Joana or for her parents to get used to living in the United States? Explain your answer.

Paragraph 5
9. Where does Joana work?
10. What is her big dream?

SHARING INFORMATION

Discuss these questions in pairs or small groups.

1. Do you have a dream? What is it?
2. When you came to the United States, did you come alone or with your family? If you came with your family, who did you come with?
3. Did you know any English when you came to the United States? If so, how much? How did you learn it?
4. Do you think most of your teachers are understanding?
5. Do many of the students in your school come from your country? If so, does this make it more difficult to learn English? Explain your answer.
6. Do the students in your school mix much—do they talk to and make friends with students from other countries?
7. What was the most difficult thing for you to get used to in going to school (or work) in the United States?

STORY COMPLETION

Going to College

Maria came to the United States when she was ten. She started college last September and wants to be a Spanish teacher when she graduates.

Complete the story with these words.

mixed	noisy	lonely	got used to
at first	few	mind	dream

Maria was born in Puebla, Mexico and came to the United States with her mom and dad when she was ten. She learned English well in a _____ years, and now her _____ is to graduate from college and teach Spanish.

Maria entered college last September. _____, college was very difficult. She missed her family and friends, and was _____. But Maria _____ with the other students, made new friends, and soon _____ living away from home.

Maria has to study a lot more than she did in high school, but she doesn't _____. She likes to study. However, the dormitory she lives in is _____, so she goes to the library to study.

A Diamond Ring

WORD BANK

1. **accountant** *n.* a person who keeps and checks financial records "An <u>accountant</u> checks the company's finances every year."
2. **anymore** *adv.* from now on; from then on "Mel hurt his back and can't play basketball <u>anymore</u>."
3. **both** *pron.* or *adj.* the two of them "Sally and her brother are very good students, and <u>both</u> want to be engineers."
4. **chat** *v.* or *n.* to talk informally with another person "Tom and Sheryl are <u>chatting</u> about a movie they saw."
5. **concert** *n.* a musical event "Courtney and Scott went to a jazz <u>concert</u>."
6. **diamond** *n.* a very hard, valuable stone used in making rings (In the United States, a man usually gives a woman a *diamond* ring when he proposes.) "Roberta is wearing a beautiful <u>diamond</u> ring."
7. **join** *v.* to become a member of "Curtis <u>joined</u> the army."
8. **no longer** *idiom* not now; not anymore "Abdul <u>no longer</u> lives in New York City. He moved to Los Angeles."
9. **propose** *v.* to make an offer of marriage to someone "Victor <u>proposed</u> to Doris, and she said yes."
10. **quickly** *adv.* fast "Darren cleaned his room <u>quickly</u>."

PREVIEW QUESTIONS

Discuss these questions before reading the story.

1. Can you swim? Are you a good swimmer? Do you ever play tennis? Do you play much?
2. How do a couple know they're in love?
3. When you first came to the United States, did anyone help you a lot? Who?

Joana loves to play tennis and swim, and last summer she joined a swim club. It was there that she met Chris. He's an accountant. At first, Joana and Chris were just friends, who liked to play tennis together and to chat about their jobs, but that changed quickly.

Joana began to think about Chris a lot and to feel that he was special. She couldn't wait to get to the club to talk to him. Tennis and swimming weren't so important anymore. Chris started to take her out. They went to movies, to dinner, and to concerts. They took long walks, and talked about their work, their families, their plans, and their dreams for the future.

Joana couldn't stop thinking about Chris, and he was crazy about her. There was a new light in her eyes. Chris proposed to Joana, but he didn't have to. They both knew. On her 28th birthday, Chris gave her a diamond ring, and she was the happiest woman in the world.

Joana and Chris are going to get married after she graduates from law school. She's no longer the lonely little girl who couldn't speak English. She's grateful to her parents, her teachers, and the friends she made when she came to the United States.

COMPREHENSION

Answer these questions about the story. Use your own ideas to answer questions with an asterisk.

Paragraph 1

1. What did Joana do last summer?
2. Who did she meet at the swim club?
3. What is Chris?
4. What did Joana and Chris do together?

Paragraph 2

5. Why couldn't Joana wait to get to the swim club?
6. Where did Chris take her?
7. What did they talk about on their walks?

Paragraph 3

8. Why didn't Chris have to propose?
9. What did he give Joana? When?
*10. Do you think most couples know they're going to get married before there is a proposal?

Paragraph 4

*11. Why do you think Joana is waiting until after her graduation to get married?
12. Who is she grateful to?

SHARING INFORMATION

Discuss these questions in pairs or small groups.

1. Do you go to movies much? Who do you go with?
2. Do you ever go to concerts? If so, what type of concerts? Where?
3. Walking is good exercise. Do you walk much? By yourself or with someone?
4. What do you and your friends like to talk about?
5. What plans do you have for the future?
6. Do you think that most couples look and act differently when they first fall in love? Explain your answer.
7. It is usually the man who proposes. Why?
8. Some women also propose. How do you feel about that?

SENTENCE COMPLETION

Complete the sentences with these words.

joined	special	together	chat	anymore

1. Jackie and I often go shopping _____.
2. Wing doesn't work here _____. He has another job.
3. Al _____ the soccer team. He's a good player.
4. Eileen frequently calls her sister, and they _____ about their families and friends.
5. Tomorrow is a _____ day. It's my 18th birthday.

quickly	proposed	no longer	both	grateful

6. I went out with Joyce for a year before I _____ to her.
7. _____ sweaters are nice, but I'm going to buy the green one.
8. Dan called the police, and they came _____.
9. The doctor saved Donna's life, and she's very _____.
10. Dustin and Lewis had a big fight. They're _____ friends.

TRUE OR FALSE

If the sentence is true, write T. *If it's false, write* F *and change it to a true statement.*

_____ 1. Good health doesn't matter.

_____ 2. Diamonds are expensive.

_____ 3. Bossy people hate to tell others what to do.

_____ 4. Sometimes married couples have to compromise.

_____ 5. Old-fashioned teachers like noisy classrooms.

_____ 6. Big businesses don't need accountants.

_____ 7. Parties give people the opportunity to mix.

SYNONYMS

Synonyms are words that have the same or a similar meaning. Next to each sentence, write a synonym for the underlined word or words.

type	difficult	quickly	attractive
a dozen	chat	just	start

1. Your girlfriend is very <u>pretty</u>. _____
2. After class, the teacher likes to <u>talk</u> with the students. _____
3. What <u>kind</u> of food do you like? _____
4. When does the parade <u>begin</u>? _____
5. Ralph did his homework <u>fast</u> and went out to play. _____
6. I went to the store to get a loaf of bread and <u>twelve</u> rolls. _____
7. That coat is <u>exactly</u> what I want. _____
8. The history test was <u>hard</u>. _____

ANTONYMS

Antonyms are words that have opposite meanings.   In the blank spaces, write an antonym for each word.

rich	special	gain	different
noisy	sad	large	old-fashioned

1. lose   _____
2. modern   _____
3. poor   _____
4. happy   _____
5. same   _____
6. ordinary _____
7. small   _____
8. quiet   _____

5

Dogs
and Money

Man's Best Friend

★~★~★~★~★~★~★~★~★~★~★~★~★~★~★~★~★~★~★~★

 **WORD BANK**

1. **bark** *v.* or *n.* to make the sound a dog makes   "Why is the dog <u>barking</u>? Is someone at the door?"
2. **bite** *v.* or *n.* to put one's teeth into   "I'm afraid of that dog. He <u>bites</u>."
3. **golden retriever** *n.* a dog with light brown (golden) hair (*Retrievers* are very friendly and popular pets. They used to be hunting dogs.)   "We're going to get a <u>golden retriever</u>. The kids are very happy."
4. **lick** *v.* or *n.* to move one's tongue across something, for example, to *lick* a stamp   "Angelo is <u>licking</u> his ice-cream cone."
5. **pet** *v.* to touch lovingly   "Lillian is <u>petting</u> her dog."
6. **puppy** *n.* a very young dog   "My dog is only a <u>puppy</u>. She's going to grow a lot."
7. **stranger** *n.* a person one doesn't know   "I never saw that man in my life. He's a <u>stranger</u>."

PREVIEW QUESTIONS

Discuss these questions before reading the dialog.

1. What are some advantages of having a dog?
2. What are some disadvantages?

Nellie is Samir's dog. She's friendly and never bites, but she barks a lot at strangers and other dogs.

Asma: What's your dog's name?

Samir: Nellie.

Asma: Can I pet her?

Samir: Sure, she's friendly. She won't bite.

Asma: Does she bark much?

Samir: Only at strangers and other dogs.

Asma: Look, she's licking my hand.

Samir: She likes you.

Asma: How old is she?

Samir: Four months. She's still a puppy.

Asma: She's going to be a big dog.

Samir: I know. She's a golden retriever.

Asma: Someday, I'm going to get a dog.

Samir: You should. A dog is man's best friend.

COMPREHENSION

Answer these questions about the dialog. Use your own ideas to answer questions with an asterisk.

1. Why is it safe to pet Nellie?
2. Who does she bark at?
3. Why is she licking Asma's hand?
4. How old is Nellie?
5. What kind of dog is she?
6. Why should Asma get a dog?
*7. Do you think Nellie will be a good watchdog? Explain your answer.

SHARING INFORMATION

Discuss these questions in pairs or small groups.

1. Do you have a dog? If so, what kind? If not, would you like to get one?
2. Why do we call dogs "man's best friend?"
3. Do dogs need a lot of care? Explain your answer.
4. Dogs "kiss" by licking people's hands and even their faces. Some people don't mind. How do you feel about having a dog lick you?

DICTATION

1. *Listen while the teacher reads the dialog without stopping. <u>Don't write anything</u>.*

2. *The teacher will read the dialog a second time, pausing after the missing lines. <u>Write in the missing lines</u>.*

3. *The teacher will read the dialog a third time. <u>Check your work</u>.*

Asma: Can I pet Nellie?

Samir: _____

Asma: Does she bark much?

Samir: _____

Asma: Look, she's licking my hand.

Samir: _____

Asma: How old is she?

Samir: _____

Asma: She's going to be a big dog.

Samir: _____

Feeling Luc

CANDY
GUM

LOTTERY
TICKETS
SOLD HERE

WORD BANK

1. **lottery** *n.* a game of chance in which people buy tickets with numbers, hoping their numbers win (Many states in the U.S. have *lotteries.*) "If I win the <u>lottery</u>, I'll be a millionaire."
2. **quit** *v.* to leave school or a job; to stop doing something "Joe is 16 and wants to <u>quit</u> school, but his parents want him to finish high school."
3. **retire** *v.* to leave one's job, usually because of age "Vince is 65. He's going to <u>retire</u> soon."
4. **spend** *v.* to use money or time "We <u>spend</u> a lot of money at the supermarket." "I know I should <u>spend</u> more time studying."
5. **ticket** *n.* a small piece of paper with numbers used in games of chance, especially the lottery "Did you see my lottery <u>ticket</u>? I can't find it."
6. **waste** *v.* or *n.* to use money or time poorly "I <u>waste</u> a lot of time watching TV."
7. **win** *v.* to receive money or other prize in a game of chance "Robin likes to play bingo, but she doesn't <u>win</u> very often."

ESTIONS

s these questions before reading the dialog.

Do you or your parents ever buy lottery tickets? If so, how often? Did you ever win anything in a lottery?
2. Do you ever dream of winning the lottery? What are the chances of winning?

Park is going to buy a lottery ticket. His sister, Lee, thinks he has no chance of winning.

Lee: Where are you going?

Park: To buy a lottery ticket. I feel lucky.

Lee: You're wasting your time and money.

Park: Why? It's fun.

Lee: You'll never win.

Park: Maybe I will. Who knows?

Lee: How much do you spend on tickets?

Park: Only two dollars a week.

Lee: What are you going to do if you win?

Park: Buy a house, a car, and a boat.

Lee: And quit work?

Park: No, I'm too young to retire. Besides, I like my job.

Lee: Maybe I should buy a ticket.

Park: Why not? What can you lose?

Lee: A dollar.

TRUE OR FALSE

If the sentence is true, write T. *If it's false, write* F.

_____ 1. Park feels lucky.

_____ 2. Lee thinks it's a good idea to buy a lottery ticket.

_____ 3. Park likes to buy lottery tickets.

_____ 4. He spends a lot of money on lottery tickets.

_____ 5. If he wins the lottery, he's going to buy a car and stop working.

_____ 6. He thinks Lee should buy a lottery ticket.

SHARING INFORMATION

Discuss these questions in pairs or small groups.

1. Do you think buying a lottery ticket is a waste of time and money? Explain your answer.
2. How old do you have to be to buy a lottery ticket?
3. What would you do if you won a million dollars?
4. Some people who win the lottery quit their jobs. Others don't. What does it depend on?

STORY COMPLETION

A Football Coach

Jack is a high-school football coach. He likes his job, and his teams do well because they try hard.

Complete the story with these words.

wins	lucky	retire	fun
quit	if	lose	spend

Jack is the football coach at George Washington High School. He's an excellent football coach, and he likes his job a lot. He says that it's _____ to coach, especially _____ your team _____. Of course, his teams also _____, but not very often.

Jack's teams do well not because they're _____, but because they _____ a lot of time practicing, and because they never _____ trying.

Jack is 68 years old, and he's going to _____ at the end of the season. He'll miss coaching, and the players will miss him.

A Big Shot

1. **afford** *v.* to be able to pay for something "Stan wants to buy a Mercedes, but he can't <u>afford</u> it."
2. **argument** *n.* a fight with words "Courtney had an <u>argument</u> with her boss, and she almost lost her job."
3. **big shot** *idiom* a very important person "Jerry's the president of our company. He's a <u>big shot</u>."
4. **cheap** *adj.* not willing to spend money on oneself or others "I like Fred, but he's <u>cheap</u>. He hates to spend a dime."
5. **complain** *v.* to say one is unhappy about something "Betty is sick a lot, but she never <u>complains</u>."
6. **fancy** *adj.* special; not ordinary "Shawn and Ann are staying at a <u>fancy</u> hotel."
7. **make sense** *idiom* to be a good idea; to be logical "It <u>makes sense</u> to save money when you can."
8. **What's the matter?** *idiom* What's the problem? "Why is Julie going to the doctor? <u>What's the matter</u>?"
9. **upset** *adj.* or *v.* very unhappy about something "Akram can't find his new watch. He's <u>upset</u>."

PREVIEW QUESTIONS

Discuss these questions before reading the dialog.

1. Do you think that a lot of couples argue about money? Explain your answer.
2. What else do couples often argue about?

Diana is upset. She just had a fight with her husband, Wayne. She is talking to her brother, Scott, about the problem.

Scott: You look upset. What's the matter, Diana?

Diana: Wayne and I just had a big argument.

Scott: About what?

Diana: Money. He spends too much.

Scott: On what?

Diana: Fancy clothes, big cars, and expensive vacations.

Scott: Why don't you complain?

Diana: I do, but he says I'm cheap, and we argue.

Scott: Maybe he's right.

Diana: I don't think so, but I *do* like to save money.

Scott: What for?

Diana: To send the kids to college, to retire on.

Scott: That makes sense.

Diana: Yes, but he wants to be a big shot, and we can't afford it.

COMPREHENSION

Answer these questions about the dialog. Use your own ideas to answer questions with an asterisk.

1. Why is Diana upset?
2. What did Diana and Wayne argue about?
3. How does he spend his money?
4. What does he say when Diana complains?
5. Why is she saving money?
6. What does she say Wayne wants to be?
*7. Do you think that Diana is cheap? Explain your answer.

SHARING INFORMATION

Discuss these questions in pairs or small groups.

1. It's normal for married couples to argue. Why?
2. Do you argue much? Who do you argue with? Friends? Spouse? Brothers? Sisters? Parents?
3. When it comes to money, are you a saver or a spender? Are you more like Diana or Wayne?
4. What do people save money for besides college and retirement?

SENTENCE COMPLETION

Complete the sentences with these words.

argue	retire	upset	fancy	arguments

1. Irene is wearing a _____ dress to the party.
2. Abe is only 60, but he's going to _____ next year.
3. Tyrone is my best friend, but sometimes we get into _____.
4. I was in an auto accident. I'm very _____.
5. My son is 15, and he loves to _____.

matter	cheap	complain	sense	afford

6. Some students _____ about the food in the cafeteria.
7. Dorothy and I want to rent a larger apartment, but we can't _____ it.
8. Why are you walking that way? What's the _____ with your leg?
9. Tracy is sick, but she won't see a doctor. That doesn't make _____.
10. Ben never buys anything for anybody. He's _____.

New Furniture

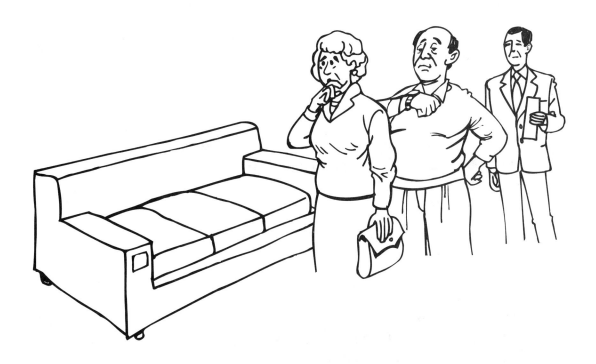

WORD BANK

1. **furniture** *n.* tables, chairs, beds, and similar items "Our new sofa cost $900. Furniture is expensive."
2. **get** *v.* to understand "Do you get what I'm saying?" "No, I don't. Explain it again."
3. **honey** *n.* a person we love a lot (We often use *honey* and words like *dear* and *darling* when talking to those we love.) "Good-bye, honey. See you later."
4. **let's = let us** *v. let's* is used to invite, to suggest "It's a beautiful day. Let's go for a walk." ("*Let's* go for a walk." = "Why don't we go for a walk?")
5. **match** *v.* or *n.* to be the same as; to go well with "Tina's red shoes and blouse match."
6. **notice** *v.* to look at and pay attention to "I noticed that Charley didn't look well."
7. **rug** *n.* a covering for a floor (*Carpet* and *rug* are synonyms.) "The rug in the bedroom is getting old."

PREVIEW QUESTIONS

Discuss these questions before reading the dialog.

1. Would you notice if the rug and furniture in a living room didn't match? Explain your answer.
2. Do you think that most husbands and wives like to shop together? Explain your answer.

 Jim wants to go to the movies with his wife, Pat, but she wants to go shopping first.

Jim: Do you want to go to the movies tonight, honey?

Pat: Sure, but we have to go shopping first.

Jim: Shopping? Again? What for?

Pat: Furniture for the living room.

Jim: But we just got a new rug for the living room.

Pat: That's why we need the new furniture.

Jim: I don't get it.

Pat: The new rug and the old furniture don't match.

Jim: Don't worry. No one will notice.

Pat: You may not, but my friends will.

Jim: Who cares if they notice?

Pat: I do. If we go now, we'll still have time for the movie.

Jim: What are we waiting for? Let's go!

TRUE OR FALSE

If the sentence is true, write T. *If it's false, write* F.

_____   1. Jim and Pat don't want to go to the movies.

_____   2. She wants to go shopping.

_____   3. Jim wants new furniture.

_____   4. Pat thinks the living room looks fine with the new rug.

_____   5. She is worried about what her friends will think.

_____   6. Pat and Jim are going shopping and to the movies.

SHARING INFORMATION

Discuss these questions in pairs or small groups.

1. Do you like to shop? For what?
2. Name a store where you shop. Why do you shop there?
3. How is shopping in the United States different from shopping in your country?
4. Do you prefer to go out to the movies, or to watch them on a VCR? Explain your answer.

MATCHING

Match the words in Column A with their definitions or descriptions in Column B. Print the letters on the blank lines.

Column A	Column B
_____ 1. bite	**A.** to go well with
_____ 2. lottery	**B.** to touch lovingly
_____ 3. match	**C.** we use our tongue to do this
_____ 4. stranger	**D.** to use money or time poorly
_____ 5. lick	**E.** a game of chance
_____ 6. furniture	**F.** a friendly dog
_____ 7. waste	**G.** a very important person
_____ 8. golden retriever	**H.** to put your teeth into
_____ 9. pet (verb)	**I.** tables, chairs, beds
_____ 10. big shot	**J.** someone I don't know

Very Different

1. **although** *conj.* in contrast to the fact that (*Although* shows that there is a contrast between two parts of a sentence.) "<u>Although</u> it's raining, I'm going for a walk."
2. **even** *adv.* surprisingly (*Even* gives emphasis to the word that follows it.) "<u>Even</u> Karen, who isn't a good student, got 100 on the test."
3. **joke** *n.* or *v.* something one says to make others laugh "Do you want to hear a good <u>joke</u>?"
4. **laugh** *v.* or *n.* to make a sound that shows we think something is funny "Everyone <u>laughed</u> at Tony's story. It was funny."
5. **mall** *n.* a shopping center with many stores "I'm going to the <u>mall</u> to buy a coat. Do you want to come?"
6. **news** *n.* a report on TV or radio about the important things happening in the world "Angela always watches the 11 o'clock <u>news</u> before she goes to bed."
7. **overweight** *adj.* weighing too much; heavier than normal "Jason is going on a diet. He's <u>overweight</u>."
8. **prefer** *v.* to like one thing better than another "Jesse likes to watch TV, but he <u>prefers</u> to listen to music."
9. **so** *conj.* for that reason "Kathy is rich, <u>so</u> she can buy anything she wants."
10. **vegetarian** *n.* a person who doesn't eat meat or fish "Tanya eats a lot of fruit, vegetables, rice, and cereal. She's a <u>vegetarian</u>."
11. **whatever** *pron.* anything "Gary lets his son do <u>whatever</u> he wants."

PREVIEW QUESTIONS

Discuss these questions before reading the story.

1. What is a vegetarian? Do you think it's healthy to be a vegetarian? Explain your answer.
2. Do you like to go to parties? Why or why not?
3. What TV programs do you watch? Do you have a favorite TV program? What is it?

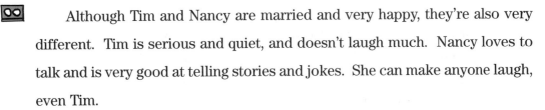

Although Tim and Nancy are married and very happy, they're also very different. Tim is serious and quiet, and doesn't laugh much. Nancy loves to talk and is very good at telling stories and jokes. She can make anyone laugh, even Tim.

Tim is tall and thin. Nancy is short and a little overweight. Tim is a vegetarian, so he never eats meat. Nancy eats anything you put in front of her. He likes to eat at home; she loves to eat out. She likes to go to parties; he prefers to stay home and read a book.

Nancy's favorite activity is shopping at malls. She buys whatever she wants and doesn't worry about how much anything costs. Tim's favorite activity is putting money in the bank and watching it grow. He saves every penny he can and buys only what he has to.

Tim watches the evening news on Channel 4 from 6:30 to 7:00, and in the fall he watches football. He loves the game. Nancy thinks the news is boring and she hates football, but she watches a lot of movies and talk shows.

COMPREHENSION

Answer these questions about the story. Use your own ideas to answer questions with an asterisk.

Paragraph 1
1. What doesn't Tim do much?
2. What does Nancy do very well?

Paragraph 2
3. What does Nancy eat?
4. Where does Tim like to eat? And Nancy?
*5. Why do you think he likes to eat at home, and she likes to eat out?

Paragraph 3
6. Where does Nancy like to shop?
7. What does she buy?
8. What is Tim's favorite activity?
*9. How do you think he feels about the way she spends money? Explain your answer.

Paragraph 4
10. What does Tim watch on TV in the fall?
11. How does Nancy feel about the news? And about football?
12. What kind of programs does she like?

SHARING INFORMATION

Discuss these questions in pairs or small groups.

1. Do you think most married couples are different or alike?
2. Are you good at telling stories and jokes?
3. Are you more of a talker or a listener?
4. Do you shop much at malls? If so, which is your favorite?
5. Do you think a lot before you decide to buy something, or do you buy things quickly?
6. Do you often watch the news on TV? Do you think the news is interesting or boring?
7. Do you frequently watch movies on TV? And talk shows?

STORY COMPLETION

A Cashier and a Cook

Jean and Glenn want to buy a house. She's a cashier, and he's a cook at a restaurant. He loves to cook, and he loves to eat. That's why he weighs so much.

Complete the story with these words.

prefers	overweight	so	laughs
boring	news	whatever	mall

Jean and Glenn are married and live in an apartment, but they plan to buy a house. They don't have enough money yet, but they save what they can and put it in the bank.

Jean works as a cashier at the _____. Her job is _____, but she needs the money.

Glenn is a cook at a French restaurant. He loves to cook and to eat. He eats _____ he wants, and he's at least 40 pounds _____. Jean wants him to go on a diet, but he _____ at the idea.

After dinner, Jean and Glenn watch the _____. Jean likes Channel 2; Glenn _____ Channel 5. _____ they compromise. One week they watch Channel 2, and the next week Channel 5.

Mark, Emily, and Midnight

WORD BANK

1. **black Lab = black Labrador retriever** *n.* a large black dog—it used to be a hunting dog "Black Labs are friendly and smart. They make great pets."
2. **check** *n.* or *v.* a watch "I'm driving to Boston this afternoon, so I'm keeping a check on the weather."
3. **close** *adj.* careful "We have to take a close look at the problem."
4. **concentrate** *v.* to direct all of one's attention to something "Jacob turned off the TV so he could concentrate on his homework."
5. **feed** *v.* to give food to "It's expensive to feed a large family."
6. **insist** *v.* to say that something has to be "Mrs. Chomko insists that her children clean their rooms."
7. **jump** *v.* or *n.* to use one's legs and feet to go into the air "The basketball players jumped to get the ball."
8. **not . . . at all** *idiom* not . . . in any way "I took the medicine, but it did not help me at all."
9. **object** *v.* to be against something "Yvonne is 16 and wants to go to a concert in New York City, but her parents object."
10. **since** *conj.* because "Andy is calling the dentist since he has a toothache."
11. **tail** *n.* the part of an animal's body that extends from its rear "Our dog has a short tail."
12. **wag** *v.* to move back and forth (said mostly of a dog moving its tail) "When our dog sees someone she knows, she wags her tail."

PREVIEW QUESTIONS

Discuss these questions before reading the story.

1. What do parents worry about when their teenage children are out late at night?
2. When a 16-year-old goes out at night, by what time should he or she be home?
3. Do you like soccer? Is it a popular sport in your country?

Tim and Nancy have two children. Mark is 16, and Emily is 14. Nancy worries about the children more than Tim does. She keeps a close check on where they're going and who they're with. When Mark goes out at night, she insists that he be home by 11:30, or 12:00 at the latest.

Mark is an excellent soccer player, and Emily is very good at basketball. Both parents go to all their games, but Nancy spends her time at the games chatting with the other parents. Tim concentrates on the games and doesn't miss anything that Mark or Emily are doing.

Nancy loves animals, especially dogs, but Tim doesn't like dogs at all. However, he doesn't object to the fact that Nancy has a black Lab since she walks, feeds, and takes care of him. His name is Midnight.

When Nancy comes home from work, Midnight is so happy. He wags his tail, jumps up on her, and licks her hands. When Tim comes home, Midnight looks up, but his tail doesn't move, and he doesn't even get up. He doesn't pay any attention to Tim because Tim doesn't pay any attention to him.

COMPREHENSION

Answer these questions about the story. Use your own ideas to answer questions with an asterisk.

Paragraph 1

    1. What does Nancy check closely?
    2. When Mark goes out, what time does he have to be home?
  *3. How do you think he feels about having to be home by 11:30 or 12:00? Explain your answer.

Paragraph 2

    4. What sport is Mark good at? And Emily?
    5. How does Nancy spend her time at the games?

Paragraph 3

    6. How does Nancy feel about dogs? How does Tim feel about them?
    7. Why doesn't he object to her having a dog?
  *8. Why do you think they named the dog Midnight?

Paragraph 4

    9. What does Midnight do when Nancy comes home?
  10. Why doesn't he pay attention to Tim?

SHARING INFORMATION

Discuss these questions in pairs or small groups.

1. How important is it that parents keep a close check on where their teenage children are and who they're with? Explain your answer.
2. Do you think most parents have a time by which their teenage children have to be home? Should they? Explain your answer.
3. Soccer is the most popular sport in the world, but basketball is more popular in the United States. Which do you think is more interesting? Why?
4. Why is it good for teenagers to participate in sports?
5. How important is it that parents show interest in their children's activities? Explain your answer.
6. Do you like animals? Are you more like Nancy or Tim?
7. If you have a dog or cat at home, does it have one person it likes best? If so, why?

SENTENCE COMPLETION

Complete the sentences with these words.

both	feed	insisted	close	concentrate

1. The boss keeps a _____ watch on the workers.
2. In the winter, we always _____ the birds.
3. It's easier to _____ when it's quiet.
4. Todd _____ on paying for my dinner.
5. We have two children, and _____ are in college.

objected	at all	since	jumped	check

6. I'm keeping a _____ on the time. I don't want to be late.
7. Rita didn't buy the coat _____ it was very expensive.
8. I wanted to invite 50 people to the party, but my wife _____, so I invited 25.
9. Shane _____ into the pool.
10. We didn't like the movie _____.

TRUE OR FALSE

If the sentence is true, write T. *If it's false, write* F *and change it to a true statement.*

_____ 1. The dog is five weeks old; he's still a puppy.

_____ 2. The rich can afford to travel.

_____ 3. Cheap people like to give big tips.

_____ 4. It's smart to waste money.

_____ 5. Friendly dogs bite.

_____ 6. A lot of people complain about the weather.

_____ 7. Many workers retire at 30.

SYNONYMS

Synonyms are words that have the same or a similar meaning. Next to each sentence, write a synonym for the underlined word or words.

rug	prefer	upset	puppy
honey	since	get	match

1. Ray didn't get the job he wanted. He's <u>very unhappy</u>. _____
2. Tiffany isn't going to the party <u>because</u> she's sick. _____
3. Scott's tie doesn't <u>go well with</u> his shirt. _____
4. I like the color of your new <u>carpet</u>. _____
5. Did you <u>understand</u> that joke? _____
6. I love you a lot, <u>dear</u>. _____
7. Max is a <u>very young dog</u>. _____
8. Which jacket do you <u>like better</u>? _____

ANTONYMS

Antonyms are words that have opposite meanings. In the blank spaces, write an antonym for each word.

laugh	new	buy	more
tall	spend	in front of	take care of

1. less _____
2. behind _____
3. short _____
4. old _____
5. neglect _____
6. save _____
7. sell _____
8. cry _____

6

Food

I'm Starving

~*

WORD BANK

1. **basement** *n.* the room or rooms in a house that are below street level "We have a washer and dryer in the <u>basement</u>."
2. **disturb** *v.* to break in on a person who is doing something; to interrupt "Melissa is writing a report. Don't <u>disturb</u> her."
3. **fix** *v.* to take something that is not working, for example, a TV set, and make it work; to repair "The mechanic is <u>fixing</u> my car."
4. **relax** *v.* to rest; to stop worrying "When Lou comes home from work, he reads the newspaper and <u>relaxes</u>."
5. **starve** *v.* to be very hungry "I didn't eat lunch; I'm <u>starving</u>."

PREVIEW QUESTIONS

Discuss these questions before reading the dialog.

1. Can you cook? Do you like to cook?
2. How often do you cook?

Nick and Carol are married. Their son, Ryan, is 18 and likes to cook. Nick is getting hungry.

Nick: Carol! Carol!

Carol: I'm in the kitchen.

Nick: Are you cooking dinner?

Carol: No, I'm on the phone.

Nick: I hate to disturb you, but I'm getting hungry.

Carol: Ryan is cooking tonight, dear.

Nick: Ryan! Ryan!

Ryan: I'm in the basement.

Nick: What are you doing?

Ryan: Fixing my bike.

Nick: That's great, but I'm starving.

Ryan: Relax, Dad. I'm coming.

Nick: What are you cooking tonight?

Ryan: Your favorite. Spaghetti and meatballs.

COMPREHENSION

Answer these questions about the dialog. Use your own ideas to answer questions with an asterisk.

1. What is Carol doing?
2. Why does Nick want to eat soon?
3. Who is cooking tonight?
4. Where is Ryan?
5. What is he doing?
6. What is he going to cook?
*7. Do you think Nick ever cooks? Explain your answer.

SHARING INFORMATION

Discuss these questions in pairs or small groups.

1. Some men cook a lot. Others don't cook at all. What is the situation in your home?
2. In your country, do men cook much?
3. If both husband and wife are working, do you think he should share the job of cooking? Explain your answer.
4. How good are you at fixing things? Very good? Good? OK? Not Good?

DICTATION

1. *Listen while the teacher reads the dialog without stopping.* <u>*Don't write anything*</u>.

2. *The teacher will read the dialog a second time, pausing after the missing lines.* <u>*Write in the missing lines*</u>.

3. *The teacher will read the dialog a third time.* <u>*Check your work*</u>.

Nick: I hate to disturb you, but I'm getting hungry.

Carol: _____

Nick: Ryan! Ryan!

Ryan: _____

Nick: What are you doing?

Ryan: _____

Nick: That's great, but I'm starving.

Ryan: _____

Nick: What are you cooking tonight?

Ryan: _____

More Chicken!

1. **mood** *n.* the way a person feels   "Since Tina is in a good <u>mood</u>, I'm going to ask her to help us."
2. **nonsense** *n.* actions or words that are foolish, that don't make sense   "Jason was throwing paper balls in our history class. The teacher told him to stop the <u>nonsense</u>."
3. **probably** *adv.* almost certainly; likely   "I'm <u>probably</u> going to the play."
4. **then** *adv.* in that case; if that is true   "If you're sick, <u>then</u> you should stay home and rest."
5. **tired of** *adj.* not interested in anymore   "Barbara is <u>tired of</u> working as a cashier." "I'm <u>tired of</u> hamburgers."

PREVIEW QUESTIONS

Discuss these questions before reading the dialog.

1. Do you eat a lot of chicken? Do you like it?
2. Do you think that it's easy to cook chicken? Explain your answer.

Sara is cooking chicken for dinner. Her husband, Pete, says that he's tired of chicken.

Pete: What's for dinner tonight, dear?

Sara: Chicken.

Pete: Chicken, chicken, and more chicken! Why do we have so much chicken?

Sara: I like chicken.   Besides, it's easy to cook.

Pete: Well, I'm tired of chicken.

Sara: And I'm tired of cooking. Maybe you should cook.

Pete: You know I can't cook.

Sara: Nonsense! You can try. A lot of men cook today.

Pete: Some do, but not me.

Sara: Then keep quiet and eat your chicken.

Pete: Let's not argue.

Sara: OK. How was work today?

Pete: Terrible! And I'm in a bad mood.

Sara: Maybe that's why you're complaining about the chicken.

Pete: Probably.

TRUE OR FALSE

If the sentence is true, write T. *If it's false, write* F.

_____ **1.** Sara cooks chicken because her husband, Pete, likes it.

_____ **2.** He complains about dinner.

_____ **3.** Sara suggests that he help with the cooking.

_____ **4.** He says that he's a good cook.

_____ **5.** He wants to stop arguing.

_____ **6.** He had a good day at work.

SHARING INFORMATION

Discuss these questions in pairs or small groups.

1. There are many ways to cook chicken. Name some.
2. How do you like your chicken?
3. Name some things that put you in a good mood.
4. Name some things that put you in a bad mood.

STORY COMPLETION

A Principal, Teachers, and Students

Mr. Green is the principal of a large high school. He is unhappy with the teachers who are always telling him how bad their students are.

Complete the story with these words.

tired of	**argue**	**so**	**mood**
nonsense	**besides**	**probably**	**complaining**

Mr. Green is the principal of Lincoln High School. He's friendly and is usually in a good _____, but not today. He has a bad headache. _____, he's _____ listening to the teachers who are always _____ about their students.

After he listens to these teachers, he tells them that their students aren't _____ bad. The teachers think that's _____, and most of them feel that Mr. Green _____ just doesn't want to be bothered.

However, the teachers don't _____ with Mr. Green. After all, he's the principal.

The Salsa Is Hot

SALAD

SALSA

WORD BANK

1. **nachos** *n.* a popular Mexican-American food—small tortillas (thin hard "bread" made of cornmeal or flour) with cheese and/or salsa "This restaurant has great <u>nachos</u> with lots of cheese."
2. **salsa** *n.* a red sauce made of tomatoes, onions, and peppers—it's usually spicy "I love <u>salsa</u>, but it's not good for my stomach."
3. **spicy** *adj.* having a lot of spice, especially hot spice (Pepper and chili powder are examples of *spices*. We add *spice* to food to make it taste better.) "The tomato sauce on the spaghetti is too <u>spicy</u> for me."
4. **stand** *v.* to accept something unpleasant; to tolerate (*Stand* is often used in negative sentences with *can't*.) "Anne can't <u>stand</u> rock music."
5. **taco** *n.* a popular Mexican-American food—a tortilla that is filled with meat, cheese, and vegetables "This <u>taco</u> has too much lettuce and not enough meat."
6. **Taco Bell** *n.* a fast-food restaurant that serves Mexican-American food "Let's eat at <u>Taco Bell</u> for a change."
7. **warn** *v.* to say that something is dangerous, difficult, or unpleasant "The doctor <u>warned</u> me to stop smoking."

PREVIEW QUESTIONS

Discuss these questions before reading the dialog.

1. Do you like Mexican-American food, for example, tortillas, tacos, and nachos?
2. Do you ever eat at Taco Bell? Often?

Paul and his cousin Erica are driving from Philadelphia to Boston. They're thinking of stopping to eat.

Paul: I'm hungry.

Erica: So am I. Let's stop at McDonald's.

Paul: No, I had a hamburger for lunch.

Erica: Do you like Mexican food?

Paul: I love it.

Erica: How about stopping at Taco Bell?

Paul: Great! What are you getting?

Erica: Tacos and a salad. And you?

Paul: Nachos with lots of cheese and salsa.

Erica: I'm warning you—the salsa is hot.

Paul: That's OK. I like spicy food. The hotter, the better.

Erica: Not me. I can't stand spicy food.

Paul: Are you sure you want to stop at Taco Bell?

Erica: Sure. Tacos aren't spicy.

COMPREHENSION

Answer these questions about the dialog. Use your own ideas to answer questions with an asterisk.

1. Why doesn't Paul want to stop at McDonald's?
2. Does he like Mexican food?
3. What is Erica getting at Taco Bell?
4. What is Paul getting?
5. What warning does Erica give him?
6. Does he like spicy food? Does she?
*7. Do you think that she eats at Taco Bell often? Explain your answer.

SHARING INFORMATION

Discuss these questions in pairs or small groups.

1. Do you like spicy food? Does it ever bother you?
2. Name some foods that are popular in your country.
3. In what way is the food you eat in the United States different from what you ate in your country?
4. Is food more expensive in the United States or in your country?

SENTENCE COMPLETION

Complete the sentences with these words.

stand	taco	so	warned	salsa

1. This _____ tastes good. I'm going to get another one.
2. My friend _____ me not to drink and drive.
3. Phil can't _____ cold weather. That's why he's moving to Florida.
4. _____ is Latin food and also a Latin dance.
5. Sharon watches a lot of TV, and _____ do I.

nachos	how about	better	spicy	let's

6. Some Indian food is _____, and some is not.
7. _____ apple pie for dessert?
8. It's getting late. _____ go.
9. _____ are my favorite snack.
10. The sooner we get home, the _____.

The C.I.A.

WORD BANK

1. **C.I.A.** *abbreviation* = Central Intelligence Agency—an agency of the United States government that secretly collects information about other countries "Beth works for the <u>C.I.A.</u> It's a dangerous job."
2. **cheap** *adj.* not costing much "Sugar is <u>cheap</u>."
3. **chef** *n.* a cook at a restaurant, especially the head cook "Tyler is a <u>chef</u> at an expensive restaurant in San Francisco, and he makes a lot of money."
4. **culinary** *adj.* having to do with the kitchen or cooking "If you want to be a professional cook, you should go to a <u>culinary</u> school."
5. **institute** *n.* a school that specializes, often in one subject, for example, computers or science "The Chubb <u>Institute</u> is a leader in computer training."
6. **public** *n.* or *adj.* everyone; all of the people "The <u>public</u> has a right to know how the government spends its tax money."
7. **spy** *n.* or *v.* a person who works for one country, collecting secret information about another country "During World War II, the United States had <u>spies</u> in Germany and Italy."
8. **train** *v.* to teach people how to do a job by giving them practice "The police department <u>trains</u> its officers before they start work."

PREVIEW QUESTIONS

Discuss these questions before reading the dialog.

1. Did you know that there are schools just to teach people how to cook?
2. How much does a diploma from a cooking school help a person get a job as a cook? Explain your answer.

After Gary graduates from high school, he is going to study at the **Culinary Institute of America (C.I.A.)** to learn how to be a chef. His friend Lisa thinks he's going to join the **Central Intelligence Agency (C.I.A.)**.

Lisa:	What are you going to do after you graduate?
Gary:	I'm going to the C.I.A.
Lisa:	To be a spy?
Gary:	No, to learn how to cook—to be a chef.
Lisa:	You've got to be kidding.
Gary:	No, I'm not. The C.I.A. is the Culinary Institute of America.
Lisa:	I never heard of it.
Gary:	Well, it's the best cooking school in the United States.
Lisa:	How do they train you to be a chef?
Gary:	We have classes and get lots of practice cooking.
Lisa:	Who do you cook for?
Gary:	The Institute has three great restaurants.
Lisa:	Can anyone eat at them?
Gary:	Sure. They're open to the public, but they're not cheap.

TRUE OR FALSE

If the sentence is true, write T. If it's false, write F.

_____ 1. Gary wants to work for the government.

_____ 2. He is going to a special school.

_____ 3. Lisa knew nothing about the Culinary Institute of America.

_____ 4. There are better cooking schools in the U.S. than the C.I.A.

_____ 5. The C.I.A. believes a student needs experience to be a good cook.

_____ 6. It doesn't cost a lot to eat at the C.I.A.'s restaurants.

SHARING INFORMATION

Discuss these questions in pairs or small groups.

1. Do chefs at big restaurants have a difficult job? Do they have a good job? Explain your answers.
2. Women do most of the cooking at home, but the majority of chefs are men. Why is this? Do you think more women are becoming chefs now? Explain your answer.
3. Why do people eat out more often today than in the past?
4. Chefs don't need a college education. Give examples of other jobs that don't require a college education, but that people often train for at special schools.

MATCHING

Match the words in Column A with their definitions or descriptions in Column B. Print the letters on the blank lines.

Column A	Column B
_____ 1. culinary	A. to say something is dangerous
_____ 2. then	B. the way one feels
_____ 3. warn	C. small tortillas with cheese
_____ 4. nonsense	D. everyone
_____ 5. nachos	E. to teach by practice
_____ 6. spy	F. in that case
_____ 7. the public	G. a red sauce
_____ 8. mood	H. an action or words that are foolish
_____ 9. salsa	I. having to do with cooking
_____ 10. train	J. a person who collects secret information

A Store and a Home

1. **convenience store** *n.* a small grocery store that opens early and closes late "Art went to the <u>convenience store</u> to get a newspaper and a can of soup."
2. **earn** *v.* to get money by working "Sandra <u>earned</u> $50,000 last year."
3. **either . . . or** *conj.* *either* is used with *or* to offer two possibilities "<u>Either</u> Kevin <u>or</u> I will drive you to the airport."
4. **goal** *n.* what a person plans to do; an aim "Sue's <u>goal</u> is to get a better job."
5. **groceries** (plural) *n.* food and other things we use at home, for example, soap and paper towels "Every Saturday morning, Cynthia buys <u>groceries</u> at the supermarket."
6. **grocery store** *n.* a store that sells food and other things we use at home "Sal went to the <u>grocery story</u> to get potatoes, cereal, and ice cream."
7. **hurry** *n.* or *v.* to move fast (verb); the act of moving fast (noun) "I can't wait for you. I'm in a <u>hurry</u>." "The doctor is <u>hurrying</u> to the hospital."
8. **language** *n.* a system of communicating by words "The United States, England, and Australia use the English <u>language</u>."
9. **midnight** *n.* twelve o'clock at night; the middle of the night "I have to be home by <u>midnight</u>."
10. **neighborhood** *n.* a small area of a city or town "There are a lot of nice houses in our <u>neighborhood</u>."
11. **sacrifice** *n.* or *v.* the loss or giving up of something of value to get something else "Craig and Joan are making many <u>sacrifices</u> to send their children to college."
12. **vacation** *n.* a time of rest from work or school "Enjoy your <u>vacation</u>!"

PREVIEW QUESTIONS

Discuss these questions before reading the story.

1. What are some of the advantages of having your own business, for example, of running a store?
2. What are the some of the disadvantages?
3. Where do you buy most of your groceries? Do you ever buy anything at a convenience store? If so, what?

Kala and Ankita Patel came to the United States from a small town in India seven years ago. Their first language is Gujarati. Kala's first job was as a waiter in an Indian restaurant. He didn't make a lot of money, but Ankita also worked part time in her cousin's grocery store.

Today Kala and his wife run a convenience store that sells newspapers, magazines, lottery tickets, milk, bread, and other groceries. It's a store where people go to buy a few things when they're in a hurry.

Kala and Ankita's store is open from six in the morning until midnight, seven days a week, 365 days a year. Either Kala or Ankita is always in the store, so they both work long hours. They haven't had a vacation since they came from India. They earn a good living from the store, but they also make a lot of sacrifices.

Last year Kala and Ankita bought a house. This was always their big goal. The house isn't large, but it's pretty and it's in a quiet neighborhood. They're very proud of their new home.

COMPREHENSION

Answer these questions about the story. Use your own ideas to answer questions with an asterisk.

Paragraph 1

1. How long ago did Kala and Ankita come to the United States?
2. What is their first language?
3. What was his first job? And hers?

Paragraph 2.

4. What does Kala and Ankita's store sell?
5. When do people go to their store?
*6. Why does a convenience store have to charge more for most of the things it sells?

Paragraph 3

7. What time does Kala and Ankita's store open? What time does it close?
8. How many days a week is their store open? How many days a year?
*9. Why do you think that either Kala or Ankita is always in the store?

Paragraph 4

10. What was Kala and Ankita's big goal?
11. Describe their house. Describe their neighborhood.
12. How do they feel about their home?

SHARING INFORMATION

Discuss these questions in pairs or small groups.

1. What is your first language? In what country or countries is it spoken?
2. Do you rent the house or apartment in which you live?
3. Does the price of a house depend a lot on its neighborhood? Explain your answer.
4. Is working in a convenience store dangerous? Explain your answer.
5. Do you think the owner of a convenience store makes much money? Explain your answer.
6. What are some of your goals in life?
7. What sacrifices will you have to make to obtain those goals?

STORY COMPLETION

A Better Place to Live

Chung lives in a small apartment in Brooklyn, New York. He wants to rent a larger apartment or buy a house.

Complete the story with these words.

either	language	grocery store	earn
midnight	goal	hurry	neighborhood

Chung lives in a small apartment in Brooklyn, New York, and his _____ is to move to a nicer _____. He wants _____ to rent a bigger apartment or to buy a house.

Chung works in a _____ from ten in the morning to ten at night. He doesn't get to bed until _____.

He's also studying English so he can get a better job and _____ more, but English is very difficult. It's not a _____ that you can learn in a _____.

Growing Up in America

1. **emphasize** *v.* to give special attention to "The first-grade teacher <u>emphasizes</u> reading."

2. **engineering** *n.* the science and profession of planning and building roads, bridges, machines, etc. "You have to be good in math to study <u>engineering</u> in college."

3. **grade** *n.* the level of a class in a school "My daughter is in the eighth <u>grade</u>, and my son is in the third <u>grade</u>."

4. **importance** *n.* value; the fact of being important "I'm reading a book about the <u>importance</u> of exercise."

5. **interfere** *v.* to get in the way of "Drinking coffee at night <u>interferes</u> with my sleep."

6. **lifeguard** *n.* a person whose job is to watch swimmers and save them if they need help "During the summer, Travis is a <u>lifeguard</u> at Jones Beach."

7. **pediatrician** *n.* a doctor who treats children "The baby is sick, so I'm taking him to a <u>pediatrician</u>."

8. **senior** *n.* a student in the last year of high school or college "Justin is a <u>senior</u>; he'll graduate in June."

9. **wiz** *n.* a person who is very smart, especially in some field of study "Jennifer is a history <u>wiz</u>, and she got an A+ in American history."

PREVIEW QUESTIONS

Discuss these questions before reading the story.

1. Do you use a computer much? Do you like to use computers?
2. Why is it important to learn how to use computers?
3. Are you interested in sports? What sports are you interested in? Do you play or just watch?

Kala and Ankita have two children, Jayesh, who is a senior in high school, and Manda, who is in the seventh grade. Jay is very good in math and science, and is going to study engineering in college. He's also a computer wiz. Jay likes to play basketball with his friends, but sports aren't a big thing in his life.

Jay helps out at the convenience store on weekends, but his parents won't let him work on school days. The family has always emphasized the importance of education, and they don't want anything to interfere with his studies.

Manda is also an excellent student, and biology and history are her favorite subjects. Someday she hopes to be a doctor. She wants to be a pediatrician so she can help children. She knows it will take many years of hard study, but that doesn't bother her.

However, it's not all study and no play for Manda. She likes to play volleyball and is a very good swimmer. She wants to be a lifeguard when she's old enough. After school on Thursdays, Manda takes piano lessons. She loves music and spends a lot of time practicing the piano.

COMPREHENSION

Answer these questions about the story. Use your own ideas to answer questions with an asterisk.

Paragraph 1

　　1. In what subjects is Jay very good?
　　2. What does he want to study in college?
　　3. What sport does he like to play?

Paragraph 2

　　4. What does Jay do on the weekends?
　　5. Why won't his parents let him work during the week?
　*6. Do you agree that he shouldn't work during the week? Explain your answer.

Paragraph 3

　　7. What are Manda's favorite subjects?
　　8. What does she hope to be someday?
　　9. Why does she want to be a pediatrician?

Paragraph 4

　　10. What does Manda want to do when she's old enough?
　　11. What does she do after school on Thursdays?
　*12. Do you think that Manda's love of swimming and music will help her in college and medical school? Explain your answer.

SHARING INFORMATION

Discuss these questions in pairs or small groups.

1. What are your favorite subjects?
2. Do you like science? Are you good in science?
3. Why does a person need more education today than in the past?
4. Name some things that can interfere with doing well in school.
5. A doctor has to be intelligent. What else should a doctor be?
6. Do you like music a lot? What kind of music do you like?
7. What kind is popular in your country?
8. Can you play the piano? Can you play any musical instrument?

SENTENCE COMPLETION

Complete the sentences with these words.

grade	engineering	emphasizes	however	lifeguard

1. Our English teacher _____ writing.
2. You have to be a very good swimmer to be a _____.
3. The fifth _____ is going on a trip to the zoo.
4. I slept well last night. _____, I still feel tired.
5. _____ students have to study a lot.

importance	interfere	wiz	so	pediatrician's

6. Alex and Hakeem are going to the park _____ they can play tennis.
7. The parade is going to _____ with traffic.
8. There are a lot of children in the _____ office.
9. Kim is a math _____.
10. Danielle and her husband are discussing the _____ of saving money.

TRUE OR FALSE

If the sentence is true, write T. *If it's false, write* F *and change it to a true statement.*

_____ 1. Houses are cheap.
_____ 2. Chefs work in kitchens.
_____ 3. Pediatricians take care of old people.
_____ 4. A wiz is very smart.
_____ 5. Taco Bell is a good place to get spaghetti.
_____ 6. Spies like the public to see what they're doing.
_____ 7. TV can interfere with homework.

SYNONYMS

Synonyms are words that have the same or a similar meaning. Next to each sentence, write a synonym for the underlined word or words.

relax	importance	excellent	goal
disturb	chef	hurry	fix

1. Mr. Ramos and Ms. Redmond are <u>very good</u> teachers.
   _____

2. I can <u>repair</u> the chair. _____
3. Everyone understands the <u>value</u> of good health. _____
4. Please don't <u>bother</u> Hillary. She's sleeping. _____
5. Why are you in a <u>rush</u>? We're early. _____
6. On weekends, Ed likes to <u>rest</u>. _____
7. Dennis is a <u>cook at a restaurant</u>. _____
8. Ashley's <u>aim</u> is to save $300 a month. _____

ANTONYMS

Antonyms are words that have opposite meanings. In the blank spaces, write an antonym for each word.

cheap	stop	pretty	basement
best	work	first	after

1. ugly _____
2. play _____
3. expensive _____
4. attic _____
5. start _____
6. before _____
7. worst _____
8. last _____

7

Cars and Accidents

An Accident

1. **damage** *n.* or *v.* a loss of value "The wind and the rain did a lot of <u>damage</u> to our garden."
2. **fault** *n.* responsibility for doing something wrong "It's your <u>fault</u> that you got an F. You never study."
3. **insurance** *n.* a contract between a company and the owner of a car—the owner pays the company, and it agrees to pay for any damage to the car "You shouldn't drive a car without <u>insurance</u>."
4. **lie** *v.* or *n.* to say what one knows isn't true (The present participle of *lie* is *lying*.) "Joe says he didn't take the money, but I think he's <u>lying</u>."
5. **over** *prep.* more than "There were <u>over</u> 50,000 people at the concert."
6. **speed** *v.* or *n.* to drive very fast; to drive faster than the law allows "Judy got a ticket for <u>speeding</u>. She was going 70 miles an hour."
7. **trouble** *n.* a difficult situation "Adam was late for work again. He's in <u>trouble</u>."
8. **truth** *n.* the facts; what is true "I hope you're telling the <u>truth</u>."
9. **worse** *adj.* the comparative of the adjective *bad* "I have a bad cold, but yours is <u>worse</u>."

PREVIEW QUESTIONS

Discuss these questions before reading the dialog.

1. Did you think that teenage drivers have a lot of accidents? If so, why?
2. Why is it so expensive to repair a car?

 Frank is a senior in high school. He is telling his girlfriend, Jamie, about the accident he had.

Frank: I'm in big trouble.

Jamie: What's the problem?

Frank: I had an accident in my dad's car.

Jamie: Did anyone get hurt?

Frank: No, but you should see his car.

Jamie: How much damage did you do?

Frank: A lot. It'll cost over $2,000 to fix it.

Jamie: Was the accident your fault?

Frank: Yes, I was speeding.

Jamie: You have insurance, don't you?

Frank: Sure, but my dad's going to be very angry.

Jamie: What are you going to tell him?

Frank: The truth. Lying only makes things worse.

Jamie: You're right.

COMPREHENSION

Answer these questions about the dialog. Use your own ideas to answer questions with an asterisk.

1. What happened to Frank?
2. How much will it cost to fix the car?
3. Why was the accident Frank's fault?
4. Does he have insurance?
5. How is his father going to react?
6. Why is Frank going to tell the truth?
*7. What do you think his father is going to say?

SHARING INFORMATION

Discuss these questions in pairs or small groups.

1. How old do you have to be to get a driver's license in your state? Is that too young? Explain your answer.
2. What does a person have to do to get a driver's license?
3. Will Frank's dad have to pay more for his auto insurance? Explain your answer.
4. Do you think Frank will stop speeding because of his accident? Explain your answer.

DICTATION

1. *Listen while the teacher reads the dialog without stopping. Don't write anything.*

2. *The teacher will read the dialog a second time, pausing after the missing lines. Write in the missing lines.*

3. *The teacher will read the dialog a third time. Check your work.*

Jamie: What's the problem?

Frank: _____

Jamie: Did anyone get hurt?

Frank: _____

Jamie: How much damage did you do?

Frank: _____

Jamie: Was the accident your fault?

Frank: _____

Jamie: You have insurance, don't you?

Frank: _____

911

WORD BANK

1. **blanket** *n.* a soft covering used to keep people warm   "It's going to be very cold tonight. I put another <u>blanket</u> on my bed."
2. **bleed** *v.* to lose blood   "Shirley's hand is <u>bleeding</u>. She cut it with a knife."
3. **block** *n.* the area or distance from one street to the next   "We live three <u>blocks</u> from the high school."
4. **bottom** *n.* the lowest part of something   "It's a mile from the <u>bottom</u> of the mountain to the top."
5. **breathe** *v.* to take air into the lungs and let it out   "The cold medicine helps me to <u>breathe</u>."
6. **conscious** *adj.* awake; knowing what is happening   "Were you <u>conscious</u> during the operation?"
7. **hill** *n.* an area that is higher than the land around it (A *hill* is not as high as a mountain.)   "The hotel is on a <u>hill</u>."
8. **on the way** *idiom* coming   "I called for a taxi, and it's <u>on the way</u>."
9. **ride** *v.* or *n.* to go from one place to another by bicycle, horse, car, bus, or plane   "Rudy likes to <u>ride</u> his bike to work."

PREVIEW QUESTIONS

Discuss these questions before reading the dialog.

1. Do you have a bike? Do you ride it much?
2. How dangerous is it to ride a bike? Explain your answer.

Don is riding a bike and hits a tree. Don's sister, Kate, runs to tell their mother. The mother goes to help Don, and Kate calls 911 for help. Jeff answers her call.

Kate: Mom, Mom, come quickly! Don's hurt!

Mom: What happened?

Kate: He was riding his bike down the hill and hit a tree.

Mom: Call 911! I'll help Don.

Jeff: 911. Jeff speaking. How can I help you?

Kate: My brother was riding a bike and hit a tree. He cut his head. He's bleeding.

Jeff: Is he conscious?

Kate: No, but he's breathing.

Jeff: What's your address?

Kate: 201 Jefferson Street.

Jeff: And where's your brother?

Kate: Half a block from here at the bottom of the hill.

Jeff: OK. Put a blanket on him, but don't move him.

Kate: Please hurry!

Jeff: Help is on the way! We'll be there quickly!

TRUE OR FALSE

If the sentence is true, write T. *If it's false, write* F.

_____   1. Don was riding his bike and was hit by a car.

_____   2. His mom called 911.

_____   3. Don cut his head.

_____   4. He was conscious after the accident.

_____   5. Jeff told Kate not to move Don.

_____   6. Jeff said help would be there soon.

SHARING INFORMATION

Discuss these questions in pairs or small groups.

1. Did you ever get hurt when riding a bike or playing? If so, describe what happened.
2. Did you ever call 911? If so, why?
3. Do you wear a helmet when you ride a bike? If not, why not?
4. Some states have laws about wearing a helmet when riding a bike. Does your state? Is the law only for children?

STORY COMPLETION

A Broken Arm and Nose

Reggie was going to the park on his motorcycle when he hit a parked car. Mrs. Thompson, who saw the accident, called the police and went to help Reggie.

Complete the story with these words.

breathe	conscious	riding	hurried
on the way	hill	quickly	bleeding

Reggie was _____ his motorcycle to the park and was going down a big _____ when he lost control of the motorcycle and hit a parked car.

He broke his nose and his right arm. His nose was also _____ a lot, and this made it harder for him to _____.

Mrs. Thompson, who lives on the hill, saw the accident. She called the police _____ and _____ to help Reggie. Fortunately, he was _____ when she got to him. She told him that an ambulance was _____.

Quiet, Roomy, and Safe

1. **brake** *n.* or *v.* the part of a car that slows and stops it "Don't worry. Our car has good <u>brakes</u>."
   anti-lock brakes *n.* special brakes that help a car stop safely when it stops suddenly, or on snow or ice "My car has <u>anti-lock brakes</u>."
2. **comfortable** *adj.* nice to sit on; relaxing "The sofa is very <u>comfortable</u>."
3. **crash** *n.* or *v.* an accident in which a car, train, or plane hits something with great force "Sixty people were killed in the plane <u>crash</u>."
4. **hop** *v.* or *n.* to jump a short distance on one leg: to get in "Joshua hurt his left foot. That's why he's <u>hopping</u> across the room." "Marie <u>hopped</u> in the car."
5. **room** *n.* space "The kitchen has <u>room</u> for a small table."
6. **roomy** *adj.* having a lot of space; having a lot of room "I like these closets. They're <u>roomy</u>."
7. **standard** *adj.* not extra "Air-conditioning was <u>standard</u> on my car."
8. **trunk** *n.* the area in the back of a car where we put things "Ron put the groceries in the <u>trunk</u> of the car."
9. **worth** *prep.* or *n.* having a value equal to the money paid; equal in value to "The watch costs $100, but it's <u>worth</u> it."

PREVIEW QUESTIONS

Discuss these questions before reading the dialog.

1. Do you drive? If not, how do you get where you want to go?
2. When people buy a car, they look for power, safety, and comfort. Which do you think is the most important? Explain your answer.

Mi Cha is talking to her brother, Kim Woo, about his new car. He likes it very much, and so does she.

Mi Cha:	How do you like your new Camry?
Kim Woo:	I love it. It's quiet, roomy, and safe.
Mi Cha:	How do you know it's safe?
Kim Woo:	The government did crash tests on it.
Mi Cha:	That's good.
Kim Woo:	Hop in and I'll give you a ride.
Mi Cha:	Thanks. These seats are comfortable.
Kim Woo:	Very, and there's lots of room in the trunk.
Mi Cha:	Did you get anti-lock brakes?
Kim Woo:	They're standard on all Camrys.
Mi Cha:	I bet the car was expensive.
Kim Woo:	Twenty-two thousand dollars.
Mi Cha:	That's a lot.
Kim Woo:	Yes, you pay a little more, but I think it's worth it.
Mi Cha:	So do I. I like the way it rides.

COMPREHENSION

Answer these questions about the dialog. Use your own ideas to answer questions with an asterisk.

1. Why does Kim Woo love his Camry?
2. How does he know it's safe?
3. How does Mi Cha describe the seats?
4. Do all Camrys have anti-lock brakes?
5. How much did the car cost?
6. What does Mi Cha like about the Camry?
*7. Do you think Kim Woo has a good job? Explain your answer.

SHARING INFORMATION

Discuss these questions in pairs or small groups.

1. How do anti-lock brakes help? In what kind of weather are they especially helpful?
2. Why is it so important to wear a seat belt? Do you always wear one?
3. It's much cheaper to buy a used car than a new one. What are some of the problems with buying a used car?
4. If you had a lot of money, what kind of car would you buy? Explain your answer.

SENTENCE COMPLETION

Complete the sentences with these words.

roomy	crash	trunk	hop in	bet

1. There was a big train _____ near Chicago.
2. It's hot. I'm going to _____ the pool and go for a swim.
3. Your apartment is _____ and very pretty.
4. I _____ you had fun at the picnic.
5. There's a tire in the _____ of the car.

comfortable	standard	brakes	worth	ride

6. Our car is getting old, and it needs new _____.
7. I'm going to _____ to work with Denise.
8. Air bags are _____ on all new cars.
9. That TV is $600. Do you think it's _____ it?
10. I like these shoes. They're very _____.

The Ax Slipped

WORD BANK

1. **ax** *n.* a tool with a long handle and metal head used to cut wood   "Al is looking for his <u>ax</u>. He is going to cut down a tree."
2. **chop** *v.* to cut wood by hitting it with an ax   "Evan is <u>chopping</u> wood for the fireplace."
3. **definitely** *adv.* clearly; without doubt   "Mary Lou is <u>definitely</u> the best player on our volleyball team."
4. **immediately** *adv.* without delay   "Come <u>immediately</u>. We need your help."
5. **pretty** (informal) *adv.* very (but usually not as strong as *very*)   "It's <u>pretty</u> cold out. I'm going to wear a hat."
6. **scar** *n.* or *v.* a mark left on one's skin from a cut   "Neil has a small <u>scar</u> on his nose."
7. **slip** *v.* or *n.* to move or fall by accident   "The glass I was holding <u>slipped</u> and fell on the floor."
8. **stitch** *n.* or *v.* the thread sewn into a cut to close it and stop the bleeding   "Fran cut her foot on a piece of glass and needed six <u>stitches</u>."
9. **yard** *n.* the area around a house   "The dog is in the <u>yard</u>."

PREVIEW QUESTIONS

Discuss these questions before reading the dialog.

1. Did you ever get a bad cut? If so, how?
2. Did you ever need stitches? How many? Why?

Bill cut his ear with an ax, and his mother had to take him to the hospital. Vicky is talking to her brother Brian. She is asking him if their brother, Bill, is home.

Vicky: Is Bill home?

Brian: No, Mom took him to the hospital.

Vicky: Why? What's wrong?

Brian: He cut his ear with the ax.

Vicky: How did that happen?

Brian: He was chopping wood in the back yard, and the ax slipped.

Vicky: How bad is the cut?

Brian: Pretty bad. We couldn't stop the bleeding.

Vicky: So he'll need stitches.

Brian: Definitely. He was lucky he didn't cut his ear off.

Vicky: He'll probably have a scar.

Brian: Probably, but don't worry. He'll be OK.

Vicky: Does Dad know?

Brian: Of course. I called him at work. He went to the hospital immediately.

TRUE OR FALSE

If the sentence is true, write T. *If it's false, write* F.

_____   1. They took Bill to the hospital in an ambulance.

_____   2. He cut his hand.

_____   3. He was chopping wood.

_____   4. He was bleeding a lot.

_____   5. Brian isn't sure that Bill will need stitches.

_____   6. Brian told his dad about the accident.

SHARING INFORMATION

Discuss these questions in pairs or small groups.

1. Do you think Bill had to stay in the hospital after he got the stitches? Explain your answer.
2. Did you ever have to go to a hospital? If so, why?
3. How long were you there?
4. How are hospitals in your country and the United States different?

MATCHING

Match the words in Column A with their definitions or descriptions in Column B. Print the letters on the blank lines.

	Column A	Column B
_____	1. blanket	A. the thread sewn into a cut
_____	2. ax	B. to move by accident
_____	3. on the way	C. equal in value to
_____	4. stitch	D. we use it to keep warm
_____	5. damage	E. they stop cars
_____	6. worth	F. a difficult situation
_____	7. speed	G. a tool to chop wood
_____	8. brakes	H. a loss of value
_____	9. slip	I. to drive very fast
_____	10. trouble	J. coming

The Titanic

Source: Culver Pictures, New York

WORD BANK

1. **couple** *n.* a man and woman who are married or considering marriage "The young <u>couple</u> are planning their wedding."
2. **crew** *n.* all who work on a ship or plane "The ship has a <u>crew</u> of 200."
3. **far** *adv.* at a great distance "It isn't <u>far</u> to the post office."
4. **honeymoon** *n.* the vacation taken by couples after they marry "Megan and Rick are going to Hawaii on their <u>honeymoon</u>."
5. **iceberg** *n.* a very large piece of ice floating in the ocean "<u>Icebergs</u> can be very dangerous."
6. **knot** *n.* a measure of the speed of a ship, about 1.15 miles an hour "The ship is going 20 <u>knots</u> an hour."
7. **luxury** *n.* something that is not necessary and gives great pleasure "Pam lives in a <u>luxury</u> apartment; she's rich."
8. **section** *n.* a separate part "Look in the biography <u>section</u> of the library, and you will find some books about Lincoln."
9. **several** *adj.* more than two, but not many "<u>Several</u> teachers are absent today."
10. **veteran** *n.* or *adj.* a person with a lot of experience "Fred has been coaching for 25 years. He's a <u>veteran</u>."
11. **voyage** *n.* a long trip on a ship "We're going on a <u>voyage</u> to England."
12. **warning** *n.* a statement that something is dangerous or difficult "Mr. Richards received a <u>warning</u> letter from school saying that his son is in danger of failing."
13. **wealthy** *adj.* or *n.* rich "The Rockefellers are <u>wealthy</u>."

146

PREVIEW QUESTIONS

Discuss these questions before reading the story.

1. What do you know about the Titanic?
2. Do you think it would be fun to cross the ocean in a big ship like the Titanic? Explain your answer.
3. Why do so few passenger ships cross the ocean today?

On April 10, 1912, the Titanic sailed from England and headed for New York City. She was the largest and safest ship in the world, and this was her first voyage. Among her 1,316 passengers were many famous and wealthy Americans, and 13 couples on their honeymoon.

First-class passengers had an indoor swimming pool, large rooms, and a fancy dining room. One couple paid $4,350 (over $70,000 in today's money) to cross the Atlantic Ocean in luxury.

Second- and third-class passengers paid much less to live in smaller rooms lower in the ship. Second-class passengers weren't allowed in the first-class sections, and third-class passengers weren't allowed in the first- or second-class sections. Most of the third-class passengers were immigrants, hoping for a new life in the United States.

On Sunday, April 14th, the Titanic received several warnings about icebergs in the area. That didn't worry Captain Smith, a veteran of 38 years at sea, or the crew. The ship continued to speed along at 22 knots an hour although it was very dark. The sea was calm and many stars were shining, but there was no moon. No one could see very far.

COMPREHENSION

Answer these questions about the story. Use your own ideas to answer questions with an asterisk.

Paragraph 1
    1. Where did the Titanic sail from?   Where was she heading?
    2. What was special about some of the passengers?

Paragraph 2
    3. What luxuries did first-class passengers have?
    4. How much did one couple pay?

Paragraph 3
    *5. Why weren't second- and third-class passengers allowed to go into the first-class sections of the Titanic?
    6. What did most third-class passengers have in common?

Paragraph 4
    7. What warnings did the Titanic receive?
    8. How fast was she going?
    *9. Why weren't Captain Smith and the crew worried?
    10. Why couldn't anyone see very far?

SHARING INFORMATION

Discuss these questions in pairs or small groups.

1. Besides icebergs, what are some other dangers to a ship crossing the ocean?
2. Some people get seasick from the motion of a ship. Do you?
3. Many passengers on the Titanic spent a lot of time playing cards. Do you like to play cards? Do you play much?
4. Second- and third-class passengers on the Titanic were not allowed to go into the first-class section. Do you think that was OK? Explain your answer.
5. One lady brought 70 dresses and 10 fur coats with her on the Titanic. At the same time, many people in 1912 didn't have enough to eat. Do we have the same problem today? Explain your answer.
6. What do you think can be done about this problem?
7. Earlier in this book, you read about another ship that sailed from England to America, the Mayflower. Compare the Mayflower and the Titanic.
8. Compare the Pilgrims and the passengers on the Titanic.

STORY COMPLETION

Acapulco, Mexico

Don and Paula are spending two weeks in a very nice hotel in Acapulco. They got married last week.

Complete the story with these words.

wealthy	**pool**	**honeymoon**	**although**
far	**luxury**	**several**	**couple**

Don and Paula are a young _____ who got married last week. They're on their _____ and are staying in a _____ hotel in Acapulco, Mexico. _____ they're not _____, they were able to save enough money to pay for the hotel.

Both of them like to swim, and they spend _____ hours a day swimming in the bay or the hotel _____.

There are some nice restaurants not _____ from their hotel. At night, they eat dinner at one of them.

Iceberg Ahead

WORD BANK

1. **ahead** *adv.* in front "There is a river a mile <u>ahead</u>."
2. **as . . . as** *conj.* to the same degree that "Milt is <u>as</u> tall <u>as</u> his cousin."
3. **bridge** *n.* the part of the ship where the officer in command stands "The captain is on the <u>bridge</u>."
4. **drown** *v.* to die from being under water "Two swimmers <u>drowned</u> in the ocean."
5. **lifeboat** *n.* a small boat carried on a larger one to use in an emergency, for example, in case of a fire "Each <u>lifeboat</u> can hold 80 people."
6. **load** *v.* or *n.* to put things or people on a ship, truck, bus, etc. "They're <u>loading</u> the truck with furniture." "They <u>loaded</u> 1,000 people on the ship."
7. **lookout** *n.* the act of watching for somebody or something "The soldiers on <u>lookout</u> were watching for the enemy."
8. **lower** *v.* to move something to a position below where it was "Please <u>lower</u> the window. I'm cold."
9. **rescue** *v.* or *n.* to save from danger "The firefighters <u>rescued</u> several people from the burning building."
10. **sink** *v.* to go to the bottom of a river, lake, or sea; to go below the surface of water "We need help. Our boat is <u>sinking</u>." (*Sunk* is the past participle of *sink*.)
11. **slow down** *v.* to go less quickly "You're driving too fast. <u>Slow down</u>!"
12. **suddenly** *adv.* happening without warning "The bus stopped <u>suddenly</u>."
13. **unsinkable** *adj.* anything that cannot sink "This ship is safe, but not <u>unsinkable</u>."

PREVIEW QUESTIONS

Discuss these questions before reading the story.

1. Imagine you are crossing the Atlantic Ocean on a large ship. Would you feel safe? Explain your answer.
2. Do you think it's possible to build a ship that's unsinkable? Explain your answer.
3. Were you ever in any type of serious accident, fire, or hurricane? If so, describe what happened.

It was almost midnight, and the Titanic was sailing peacefully to New York. Suddenly, the two sailors who were on lookout saw an iceberg directly ahead and warned First Officer Murdock, who was on the bridge. He tried to go around the iceberg, but it was too late. The right side of the Titanic hit the iceberg at 11:40 p.m. The ship began to fill up with water. Captain Smith and the crew soon knew that the Titanic was in big trouble. They radioed for help.

The crew started putting passengers in the lifeboats and lowering them into the water, but there wasn't enough room for everyone. So women and children were loaded into the boats first.

The Carpathia, a ship heading for the Mediterranean Sea, heard the Titanic's call for help and headed for the sinking ship as fast as possible. But by the time she arrived at 4:00 a.m., the Titanic had sunk.

Fortunately, the Carpathia was able to rescue 705 people from the lifeboats. All the other passengers and crew members drowned in the Atlantic Ocean.

Why didn't the Titanic slow down after receiving several warnings about icebergs? Why didn't she have enough lifeboats for everyone on the ship? The answer is clear. Everyone thought the Titanic was unsinkable.

COMPREHENSION

Answer these questions about the story. Use your own ideas to answer questions with an asterisk.

Paragraph 1

1. What did the sailors on lookout do when they saw the iceberg?
*2. What do ships have today that would warn them of an iceberg?
3. What happened to the Titanic after she hit the iceberg?

Paragraph 2

4. What did the crew start to do?
5. What was the big problem with the lifeboats?

Paragraph 3

6. What did the Carpathia do when she heard the Titanic's call for help?
*7. What danger did the Carpathia face in going to help the Titanic?
8. Before the Carpathia arrived, what happened to the Titanic?

Paragraph 4

9. How many people did the Carpathia rescue?   What happened to the others?

Paragraph 5

10. Why didn't the Titanic slow down?

SHARING INFORMATION

Discuss these questions in pairs or small groups.

1. Where can you find more information about the Titanic?
2. Do you think Captain Smith was responsible for the accident? Explain your answer.
3. If a passenger ship were sinking today, and there weren't enough lifeboats, do you think that the women would be put in the boats before the men? Should they be? Explain your answers.
4. Bigger is not always safer. A smaller ship might have been able to get around the iceberg. Why?
5. The Titanic could have stopped for the night and waited for morning. Why didn't she?
6. Plays, books, and movies about the Titanic are very popular. Why?
7. Are you safety conscious? If you're on a ship, do you check for life preservers? Does your house or apartment have smoke detectors?

SENTENCE COMPLETION

Complete the sentences with these words.

rescued	knew	lowering	lifeboats	warned

1. I _____ that Marissa would help you.
2. All large passenger ships have _____.
3. The lifeguard _____ Jane from the ocean.
4. My friend _____ me that the roads were icy.
5. Ralph is _____ the flag in front of the school.

slowed down	sink	loading	suddenly	drowned

6. They're _____ the cargo on the plane.
7. When Jonathan saw the police car behind him, he _____.
8. _____, I felt a pain in my chest.
9. If you throw the rock in the river, it'll _____.
10. Last year a girl _____ in the lake.

TRUE OR FALSE

If the sentence is true, write T. *If it's false, write* F *and change it to a true statement.*

_____ 1. Bread is a luxury.

_____ 2. Lou started teaching last year; he's a veteran teacher.

_____ 3. People chop wood with an ax.

_____ 4. Tokyo is far from New York City.

_____ 5. Hills are as tall as mountains.

_____ 6. It's foolish to drive with bad brakes.

_____ 7. A person who is drowning is in trouble.

SYNONYMS

Synonyms are words that have the same or a similar meaning. Next to each sentence, write a synonym for the underlined word or words.

right	speak	room	pretty
wealthy	over	rescue	test

1. We have a lot of <u>space</u> in our basement. _____
2. My uncle is <u>rich</u>. _____
3. I'm happy I passed the <u>exam</u>. _____
4. Your answer is <u>correct</u>. _____
5. The baby fell into the pool, but we were able to <u>save</u> her.

   _____
6. Linda is going to <u>talk</u> to you. _____
7. Gene is <u>very</u> strong. _____
8. <u>More than</u> seven million people live in New York City.

   _____

ANTONYMS

Antonyms are words that have opposite meanings. In the blank spaces, write an antonym for each word.

bottom	veteran	down	ahead
lower	fast	famous	back

1. up   _____
2. slow   _____
3. behind   _____
4. unknown   _____
5. top   _____
6. front   _____
7. raise   _____
8. beginner   _____

8

School

The First Day of School

WORD BANK

1. **beginner** *n.* a person who is beginning some activity "Scott likes to ski, but he's not very good. He's only a <u>beginner</u>."
2. **end** *v.* or *n.* to finish "What time does the movie <u>end</u>?"
3. **wow** *idiom* an informal word showing surprise "Barbara got all A's on her report card." "<u>Wow</u>! That's great!"

PREVIEW QUESTIONS

Discuss these questions before reading the dialog.

1. How do (did) you feel about the first day of school? Glad to be back? Unhappy? Explain your answer.
2. Do you get a lot of homework? Does it help you to learn? Explain your answer.

Summer is ending, and Alexi and Marina have to go back to school. They're not happy. Alexi recently arrived in the United States from Russia and doesn't know any English.

Alexi:	Tomorrow is the first day of school.
Marina:	I know, I hate to see summer end.
Alexi:	Me too.
Marina:	What grade are you entering?
Alexi:	The ninth grade.
Marina:	So it's your first year in high school.
Alexi:	Yes, and I don't know any English.
Marina:	Don't worry. They have classes for beginners.
Alexi:	That's good. How big is the high school?
Marina:	Very. It has over 2,000 students.
Alexi:	Wow! Are the teachers nice?
Marina:	Most of them are, but we get a lot of homework.
Alexi:	Oh no, I hate homework.
Marina:	So do I.

COMPREHENSION

Answer these questions about the dialog. Use your own ideas to answer questions with an asterisk.

1. When is the first day of school?
2. What does Marina hate to see?
3. What grade is Alexi entering?
4. How much English does he know?
5. How many students are in the high school?
6. What does Alexi hate?
*7. Do you think he is nervous about going to high school? Explain your answer.

SHARING INFORMATION

Discuss these questions in pairs or small groups.

1. Why is it more difficult to go to school in the United States if you don't know English? Give as many reasons as you can.
2. What are some of the advantages of a large high school? What are some of the disadvantages?
3. Do you think high schools are too big in the United States? Explain your answer.
4. Are most of your teachers nice?

DICTATION

1. *Listen while the teacher reads the dialog without stopping.* <u>*Don't write anything.*</u>

2. *The teacher will read the dialog a second time, pausing after the missing lines.* <u>*Write in the missing lines.*</u>

3. *The teacher will read the dialog a third time.* <u>*Check your work.*</u>

Alexi: Tomorrow is the first day of school.

Marina: _____

Alexi: Me too.

Marina: _____

Alexi: The ninth grade.

Marina: _____

Alexi: Yes, and I don't know any English.

Marina: _____

Alexi: That's good. How big is the high school?

Marina: _____

Old-Fashioned

Homework
page 96 – questions 1 – 10
Test – Friday
Chapter 6

∿★∿★∿★∿★∿★∿★∿★∿★∿★∿★∿★∿★∿★∿★∿★∿★∿★∿★

WORD BANK

1. **deserve** *v.* should receive; should get   "Nurses <u>deserve</u> more credit for the work they do."
2. **discussion** *n.* a talk in which people share ideas   "George and I had a long <u>discussion</u> about rock music."
3. **hide** *v.* to keep others from seeing something; to keep secret   "I tried to <u>hide</u> my anger, but it was impossible."
4. **mark** *n.* or *v.* a score on a test or in a subject   "My best <u>mark</u> was in science. I got an A."
5. **sense of humor** *n.* the ability to see and enjoy what is funny; the ability to be funny   "Jackie knows how to make people laugh. She has a great <u>sense of humor</u>."
6. **sound** *v.* to seem to be   "Your plan <u>sounds</u> good."

PREVIEW QUESTIONS

Discuss these questions before reading the dialog.

1. Do you think that students learn more from modern or old-fashioned teachers? Explain your answer.
2. Is it important that a teacher have a good sense of humor? Explain your answer.

Amy is talking to her friend Dave. They go to the same high school. They're talking about Miss Walker, Dave's history teacher.

Amy: Who's your history teacher this year?

Dave: Miss Walker. Did you ever have her?

Amy: Last year. She's old-fashioned.

Dave: What do you mean?

Amy: Not much discussion, homework every night, and lots of tests.

Dave: Does she have a sense of humor?

Amy: Yes, but she hides it at first.

Dave: How?

Amy: She doesn't smile until Thanksgiving.

Dave: Does she give good marks?

Amy: You get the mark that you deserve, nothing more and nothing less.

Dave: That's fair.

Amy: True, and she's never boring. You'll learn a lot in her class.

Dave: She doesn't sound so bad.

Amy: She's not, but you have to study and do your homework.

TRUE OR FALSE

If the sentence is true, write T. *If it's false, write* F.

_____ 1. Miss Walker is a modern teacher.

_____ 2. She believes in a lot of class discussion.

_____ 3. She has a sense of humor.

_____ 4. Her classes are interesting.

_____ 5. Amy thinks that Miss Walker is a poor teacher.

_____ 6. Miss Walker makes her students work.

SHARING INFORMATION

Discuss these questions in pairs or small groups.

1. Do you like class discussions? Do you learn much from them? Explain your answer.
2. Why would a teacher hide a sense of humor at the beginning of the school year?
3. What makes a teacher boring? What makes a teacher interesting?
4. Do you think it's easy or difficult to be a good teacher? Explain your answer.

STORY COMPLETION

Our Boss

Mr. Lee, our boss, doesn't show his feelings much, and many people don't like him. In the beginning, I didn't like him either, but now I do.

Complete the story with these words.

at first	old-fashioned	hides	fair
discussion	smiles	deserve	sense of humor

Our boss's name is Mr. Lee. Many people don't like him because he

_____ his feelings, rarely _____, and

doesn't have a _____.

_____, I didn't like him either, but now I do. I see

that he's _____ to all the workers, and at the end of the

year he gives a bonus (extra money) to those who _____ it.

Mr. Lee and I had a long _____ the other day. He has

a lot of good ideas and is not as _____ as many think.

Writing Is Tough Work

~★~

WORD BANK

1. **encyclopedia** *n.* a book, set of books, or a CD ROM with articles on many topics
   "The library has several <u>encyclopedias</u>."
2. **geography** *n.* the study of the countries, continents, oceans, rivers, and
   mountains of the world   "We're studying Africa in our <u>geography</u> class."
3. **lazybones** (*very informal*) *n.* a lazy person—a person who hates to work   "Ben
   does very little work. That's why I call him <u>lazybones</u>."
4. **surprise** *n.* or *v.* something that one does not expect   "The teacher gave us a
   <u>surprise</u> test."

PREVIEW QUESTIONS

Discuss these questions before reading the dialog.

1. Do you like to read about other countries?
2. Why is it important to know about other countries?

Mike is reading an article in an encyclopedia. He has to write a report on Japan for his geography class. He's talking to his friend Debbie.

Debbie: What are you reading?

Mike: An encyclopedia.

Debbie: What for?

Mike: A report for my geography class.

Debbie: About what?

Mike: Japan.

Debbie: That must be interesting.

Mike: Yes and no.

Debbie: What do you mean?

Mike: I don't mind reading about Japan.

Debbie: Then, what's the problem?

Mike: Writing the report. I hate to write.

Debbie: That's no surprise. Writing is tough work.

Mike: And I don't like to work.

Debbie: But you have no choice, lazybones.

Mike: I guess not.

COMPREHENSION

Answer these questions about the dialog. Use your own ideas to answer questions with an asterisk.

1. What is Mike reading?
2. Why is he reading it?
3. What's the report about?
4. Does Mike mind reading about Japan?
5. What does he mind?
6. Why does he hate to write?
*7. Do you think he's lazy? Explain your answer.

SHARING INFORMATION

Discuss these questions in pairs or small groups.

1. What do you know about Japan? (The teacher may have one or more students read about Japan in an encyclopedia and report to the class.)
2. Is writing tough work? Explain your answer.
3. Is it important to be able to write well? Explain your answer.
4. Do you write much? What do you write?

SENTENCE COMPLETION

Complete the sentences with these words.

mind	encyclopedia	means	report	tough

1. Janet is waiting for a _____ from the doctor.
2. The _____ has an interesting article about the space program.
3. It's _____ to get a good job.
4. Do you _____ taking our picture?
5. I know what the word _____, but I can't explain it.

geography	surprise	lazybones	guess	choice

6. We can go to the game or to the movies. What's your _____?
7. Mary works 12 hours a day. No one can call her _____.
8. We're studying the _____ of South America.
9. I _____ everyone had a good time at the party.
10. Roger's visit was a _____.

A Million Rules

1. **chew** *v.* to move one's teeth up and down on food   "<u>Chew</u> your food well!"
2. **detention** *n.* the keeping of students after school to punish them   "I was late for class, and Ms. Hogan gave me <u>detention</u>."
3. **enforce** *v.* to make people obey rules or the law   "It's the job of the police to <u>enforce</u> traffic laws."
4. **eraser** *n.* what we use to remove writing from a chalkboard   "There is an <u>eraser</u> on the teacher's desk."
5. **rule** *n.* or *v.* a statement that something must be done   "Our school has a <u>rule</u> that students aren't allowed to wear hats in classrooms."
6. **gum** *n.* a soft, sweet substance that we chew   "I like to chew <u>gum</u> when I drive."
7. **no wonder** *idiom* of course; naturally   (*Wonder* is a feeling of surprise.)   "You had a busy day. <u>No wonder</u> you're tired."
8. **yell** *v.* or *n.* to speak in a very loud voice; to shout   "Please don't <u>yell</u> at me!"

PREVIEW QUESTIONS

Discuss these questions before reading the dialog.

1. Many teachers punish students by giving them detention—by keeping them after school. Do you think that is a good way to punish them? Explain your answer.
2. Do you think that schools in the United States are too easy on students? Explain your answer.

Laura and Shawn are in the seventh grade and are friends. They meet in the hall after school. Shawn is not happy. He has detention.

Laura:	Where are you going?
Shawn:	I have detention with Mr. Williams.
Laura:	Not again?
Shawn:	Yes, I was throwing an eraser at Gino.
Laura:	No wonder he gave you detention.
Shawn:	Maybe I deserve it this time, but Mr. Williams is too much.
Laura:	Why do you say that?
Shawn:	He's got a million rules.
Laura:	Like what?
Shawn:	We can't talk out, we can't chew gum, we can't get out of our seats.
Laura:	A lot of teachers have rules like that.
Shawn:	Sure, but they don't enforce them the way he does.
Laura:	What does he do?
Shawn:	He yells, he gives detention, he makes us write his rules ten times.
Laura:	You're right, Mr. Williams is too much.

TRUE OR FALSE

If the sentence is true, write T. *If it's false, write* F.

_____ 1. Shawn has to stay after school.

_____ 2. Laura is surprised he got detention.

_____ 3. Mr. Williams has a lot of rules.

_____ 4. He doesn't mind if his students chew gum.

_____ 5. He insists that they obey his rules.

_____ 6. Laura likes the way Mr. Williams enforces his rules.

SHARING INFORMATION

Discuss these questions in pairs or small groups.

1. Do you think it's a good idea for a teacher to give students a list of classroom rules? Explain your answer.
2. What's the problem with students chewing gum in school?
3. Do you think it's OK for a teacher to yell at students if they're doing something wrong? Explain your answer.
4. Is there much difference between the discipline in the schools in the United States and your country? Explain your answer.

MATCHING

Match the words in Column A with their definitions or descriptions in Column B. Print the letters on the blank lines.

Column A	Column B
_____ 1. encyclopedia	A. we need teeth to do this
_____ 2. rules	B. one who hates to work
_____ 3. surprise	C. something we chew
_____ 4. chew	D. the ability to enjoy what's funny
_____ 5. eraser	E. to make others obey
_____ 6. sense of humor	F. something we don't expect
_____ 7. lazybones	G. a way to punish students
_____ 8. enforce	H. a set of books
_____ 9. gum	I. it removes writing
_____ 10. detention	J. they tell us what we must do

More Opportunities

PORTE 10

VOL 107
NEW YORK

PREVIEW QUESTIONS

Discuss these questions before reading the dialog.

1. What do you know about Haiti? Where is it? What country used to control Haiti?
2. What is the official language of Haiti? What language do most of the people speak?
3. The family in our story lives in a small village just outside of Port-au-Prince, the capital of Haiti. Do you think it's easy to find work there? Explain your answer.

Nicole was born in a small village just outside of Port-au-Prince, Haiti. Haiti was once a French colony, and most of the people speak Haitian Creole. Nicole has an older sister and three younger brothers. Nicole's father is a carpenter, but it was hard for him to find work in Haiti.

Nicole was a bright girl and loved school. Math was her favorite subject, but she also loved to read when she wasn't playing with her older sister or taking care of her younger brothers.

One day she got bad news. Her dad was going to the United States to live. He said he could find steady work there and make a lot of money. The day he flew to New York was the saddest in Nicole's life. She knew she was going to miss him a lot. He promised to bring the entire family to the United States in a few years. That only made Nicole sadder. She loved Haiti and her friends, and didn't want to leave her country.

Two years later, Nicole and the entire family flew to the United States. The children complained about going, but Nicole's mother explained that they would have more opportunities in the United States.

COMPREHENSION

Answer these questions about the story. Use your own ideas to answer questions with an asterisk.

Paragraph 1
1. How many brothers and sisters does Nicole have?
2. What is her father?

Paragraph 2
3. What was Nicole's favorite subject?
4. What did she love to do when she wasn't playing with her older sister or taking care of her younger brothers?

Paragraph 3
5. What bad news did Nicole get?
6. Why was her dad going to the United States?
*7. Why do you think he left his family in Haiti?
8. What promise did he make?

Paragraph 4
9. How did the children feel about going to the United States?
*10. How do you think Nicole's mother felt? Explain your answer.

SHARING INFORMATION

Discuss these questions in pairs or small groups.

1. Were you under 18 when you came to the United States? If so, were you unhappy about coming to live in the United States? Explain your answer.
2. Is there a big difference between the weather in Haiti and the United States? Do you think the change in weather made life more difficult for Nicole?
3. For Nicole, moving to the United States was "bad news." Think about your own life and list all the advantages and disadvantages of living in the United States.
4. The United States is a land of immigrants, but not everyone welcomes the newcomers. Do you feel that some people don't accept you because you're a newcomer? If so, how do you handle it?
5. Imagine that Nicole is about to fly from Haiti to the United States. What would you say to her? What advice would you give?
6. Nicole has three brothers and a sister. How many brothers do you have? How many sisters?
7. Where do they live?

STORY COMPLETION

Not Studying

Ted is very intelligent, but he's not doing well in school. His parents are unhappy because they know he isn't studying.

Complete the story with these words.

once	**just**	**promises**	**bright**
opportunity	**village**	**entire**	**complain**

Ted lives in a small _____ in upstate New York, and

he's very _____. He goes to high school, and he was

_____ the best student in the _____

school, but now he's _____ passing.

His parents _____ that he's not studying, and that

he's going to lose the _____ to go to a very good college.

Ted knows they're right, and he _____ to study and

get better marks.

A Dream Come True

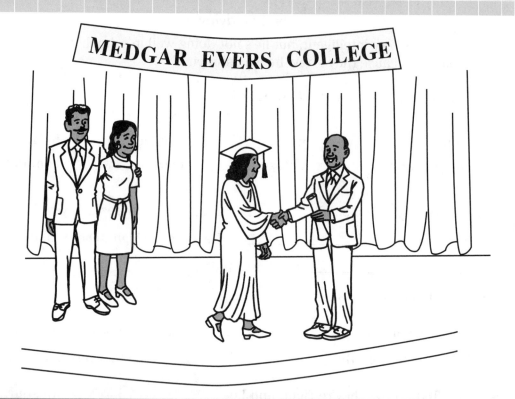

~*

WORD BANK

1. **bilingual** *adj.* able to speak and understand two languages "Jean is <u>bilingual</u>. He speaks French and English."
2. **counselor** *n.* a person whose job is to give advice "Gary and Cindy are going to a marriage <u>counselor</u>."
3. **grant** *n.* money given, often by the government, to help pay for one's education "Jerry received a <u>grant</u> to go to college."
4. **little by little** *idiom* gradually; in small amounts "Tina is very sick, but she's getting better <u>little by little</u>."
5. **respect** *n.* or *v.* a high opinion of "I have a lot of <u>respect</u> for Mrs. Bukowski; she's a very good person."
6. **scholarship** *n.* money given to help pay for one's education (*Scholarships* are grants given for high grades, financial need, and sports.) "Larry got a <u>scholarship</u> to Columbia University because he's such a good student."
7. **strict** *adj.* obeying and making others obey rules carefully "Beth's parents are very <u>strict</u>."

PREVIEW QUESTIONS

Discuss these questions before reading the dialog.

1. When a student arrives in the United States from another country, the first few weeks in school are very difficult. Why?
2. Do you think that students in your country have more respect for teachers than students in the United States? If so, why?
3. It's expensive to go to college. How can students who don't have much money go to college?

Nicole's family arrived in Brooklyn from Haiti at the end of November, and she entered the tenth grade. At first, she hated school. She didn't know anyone, and the students didn't seem to have much respect for the teachers. Fortunately, some students and one teacher spoke creole. They tried to help her.

Little by little, things got better for Nicole. She learned English, made new friends, and did well in school, especially in math.

Nicole wanted to go to college, but she didn't think the family could afford it. Then a counselor explained to her that there were scholarships and government grants, especially for students whose families don't have much money.

Four years later, Nicole graduated with high honors from Medgar Evers College. She was the first in her family ever to graduate from college. Everyone was so proud of her.

In September, she got a job as a bilingual (English/Haitian Creole) math teacher. She's very strict, but the students love her class because they learn a lot. They also know she understands them and their problems, and they can talk to her. They want to be like her. Her dream has come true.

COMPREHENSION

Answer these questions about the story. Use your own ideas to answer questions with an asterisk.

Paragraph 1

   1. Why did Nicole hate school at first?
   *2. Do you think the students didn't have much respect for the teachers, or was that just the way it seemed to Nicole? Explain your answer.
   3. Who tried to help Nicole?
   *4. How do you think they tried to help?

Paragraph 2

   5. Why did things get better for Nicole?

Paragraph 3

   6. At first, Nicole didn't think she could go to college. Why not?
   7. What did the counselor explain to her?

Paragraph 4

   8. Why was Nicole's family so proud of her? Give two reasons.

Paragraph 5

   9. What job did Nicole get?
   10. Why do the students love her class?

SHARING INFORMATION

Discuss these questions in pairs or small groups.

   1. Many immigrants go to college, but many do not. Why not? Give as many reasons as you can.
   2. What are some of the advantages of going to college?
   3. Most students go to college with the help of grants and loans. Do you have to pay back a loan? Do you have to pay back a grant?
   4. Do you take any subjects in your first language? If so, which ones? Is the textbook in your first language? Is the class taught completely in your first language, or partially in English?
   5. Do you think it's helpful for students, when they first come to the United States, to take subjects in their first language instead of English? Explain your answer.
   6. Are there teachers in your school from your country? If so, do you think they have a special understanding of you and your problems? Explain your answer.
   7. Are there teachers in your school born in other countries? If so, do you think they're stricter or easier than the teachers born in the United States? Explain your answer.

SENTENCE COMPLETION

Complete the sentences with these words.

strict	little by little	dream	scholarship	respect

1. Dan's _____ is to go to Europe.
2. Doctors deserve our _____. They work hard and have a lot of skill.
3. The principal of the high school is very _____.
4. Karen is a good student, and her family doesn't have a lot of money. That's why she's getting a _____.
5. My bank account is growing _____.

counselor	proud	grant	afford	fortunately

6. _____, I have very good health.
7. Mr. Fox is _____ of his garden.
8. Ken wants to buy a car, but he can't _____ it.
9. Leslie talked to her _____ about what subjects to take next year.
10. I need a _____ to go to college.

TRUE OR FALSE

If the sentence is true, write T. *If it's false, write* F *and change it to a true statement.*

_____ 1. Summer ends in September.

_____ 2. Students like detention.

_____ 3. There's not much information in an encyclopedia.

_____ 4. Erasers are used to remove writing.

_____ 5. Brazil was once a colony of Portugal.

_____ 6. It's difficult for bright people to learn.

_____ 7. Rules state what must be done.

SYNONYMS

Synonyms are words that have the same or a similar meaning. Next to each sentence, write a synonym for the underlined word or words.

tough	**afford**	**discussion**	**little by little**
deserve	**bright**	**yell**	**mark**

1. I had a long <u>talk</u> with my friend Allen. _____
2. Lindsay got the highest <u>grade</u> in the class on her English test. _____
3. Jay wants to buy a boat, but he can't <u>pay for</u> it. _____
4. Sometimes my parents <u>shout</u> at me. _____
5. Audrey and Terry are excellent secretaries. They <u>should get</u> more money. _____
6. It's best to lose weight <u>gradually</u>. _____
7. Pedro is very <u>intelligent</u>. _____
8. It's <u>difficult</u> to understand some people. _____

ANTONYMS

Antonyms are words that have opposite meanings. In the blank spaces, write an antonym for each word.

end	**hide**	**enter**	**night**
frequent	**high**	**over**	**old**

1. leave _____
2. low _____
3. day _____
4. less than _____
5. beginning _____
6. young _____
7. rare _____
8. show _____

Alphabetical list of the irregular verbs used in the past tense and the pages on which they first occur.

Base Form	Past	Page
begin	began	85
bring	brought	19
buy	bought	125
can	could	15
come	came	15
cut	cut	138
fly	flew	169
get	got	17
give	gave	85
go	went	61
hear	heard	41
hit	hit	37
know	knew	15
leave	left	15
lose	lost	41
make	made	37
meet	met	17
pay	paid	147
run	ran	37
say	said	169
see	saw	19
sell	sold	72
send	sent	37
speak	spoke	37
take	took	41
think	thought	59
win	won	41

Maps

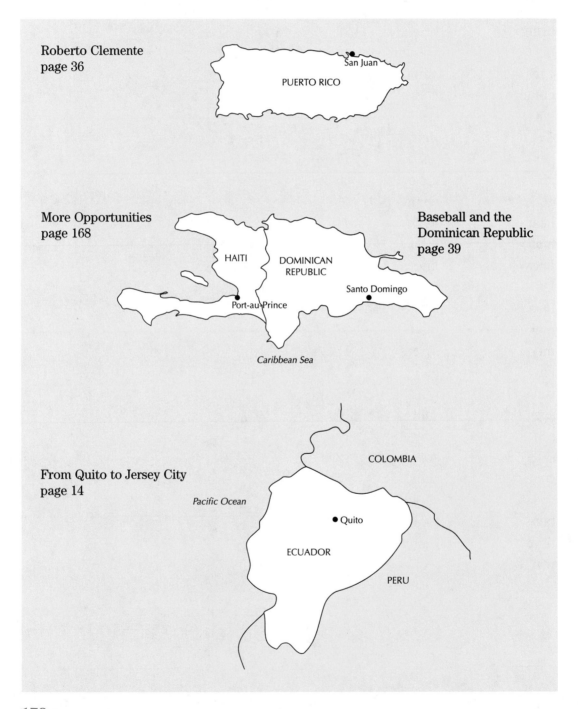

Roberto Clemente
page 36

San Juan

PUERTO RICO

More Opportunities
page 168

Baseball and the
Dominican Republic
page 39

HAITI

DOMINICAN
REPUBLIC

Port-au-Prince

Santo Domingo

Caribbean Sea

From Quito to Jersey City
page 14

COLOMBIA

Pacific Ocean

● Quito

ECUADOR

PERU

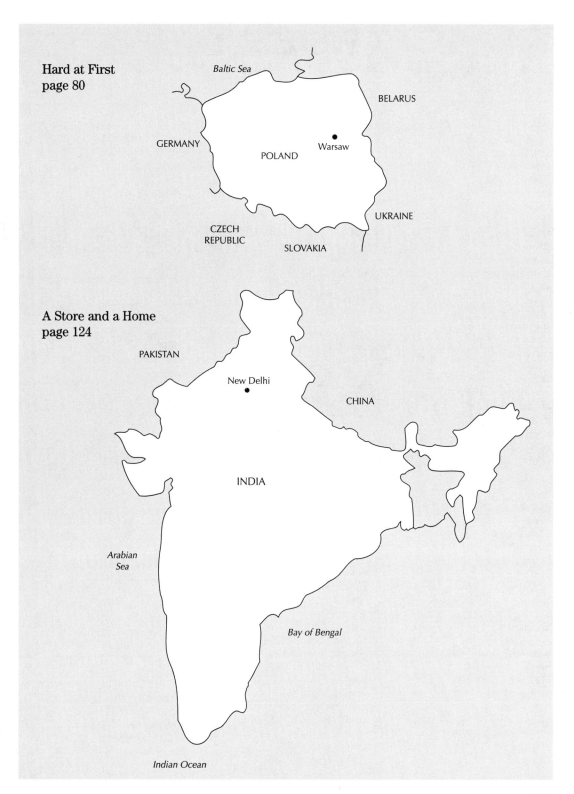

Hard at First
page 80

Baltic Sea

BELARUS

GERMANY

POLAND

Warsaw

UKRAINE

CZECH
REPUBLIC

SLOVAKIA

A Store and a Home
page 124

PAKISTAN

New Delhi

CHINA

INDIA

*Arabian
Sea*

Bay of Bengal

Indian Ocean

Word List

Alphabetical list of words defined in the **Word Bank** sections

A

a lot *idiom* 5
accountant *n.* 84
afford *v.* 96
against *prep.* 36
age *n.* or *v.* 77
ago *adv.* 14
ahead *adv.* 150
allow *v.* 5
along *prep.* 18
although *conj.* 102
angry *adj.* 68
answer *v.* or *n.* 68
anymore *adv.* 84
apply *v.* 11
argue *v.* 74
argument *n.* 96
arrive *v.* 18
as . . . as *conj.* 150
astronaut *n.* 49
at first *idiom* 80
at least *idiom* 18
attractive *adj.* 71
ax *n.* 143

B

baby-sit *v.* 5
back *n.* 27
balloon *n.* 52
band *n.* 46
bark *v.* or *n.* 90
basement *n.* 112
be crazy about *idiom* 36
beef *n.* 30
beginner *n.* 156
believe *v.* 68
believe in *v.* 30
besides *adv.* 5
bet *v.* 11
better off *idiom* 68
better (than) *adj.* 5
big shot *idiom* 96
bilingual *adj.* 172
bite *v.* or *n.* 90
black Lab = black Labrador
    retriever *n.* 106
blanket *n.* 137
bleed *v.* 137

block *n.* 137
boring *adj.* 5
borrow *v.* 55
bossy *adj.* 74
both *pron.* or *adj.* 84
bother *v.* 11
bottom *n.* 137
brake *n.* or *v.*/anti-lock
    brakes *n.* 140
breathe *v.* 137
bridge *n.* 150
bright *adj.* 168
by the way *idiom* 71

C

calm down *v.* 68
candle *n.* 49
career *n.* 36
cargo *n.* 40
carpenter *n.* 168
catch *n.* or *v.* 40
celebrate *v.* 52
chat *v.* or *n.* 84
cheap *adj.* 96
cheap *adj.* 121
check *n.* or *v.* 106
chef *n.* 121
chew *v.* 165
choice *n.* 71
chop *v.* 143
C.I.A. = Central Intelligence
    Agency *abbreviation* 121
close *adj.* 106
colony *n.* 168
comfortable *adj.* 140
company *n.* 5
complain *v.* 96
compromise *v.* or *n.* 74
concentrate *v.* 106
concert *n.* 84
conscious *adj.* 137
contract *n.* 36
convenience store *n.* 124
cookout *n.* 46
counselor *n.* 172
couple *n.* 146
courage *n.* 62
crash *n.* or *v.* 140

crash (into) *v.* or *n.* 40
creole *n.* 168
crew *n.* 146
cross *v.* 27
culinary *adj.* 121
customer *n.* 2

D

dad *n.* 8
damage *n.* or *v.* 134
dangerous *adj.* 8
decide *v.* 58
deer *n.* 30
definitely *adv.* 143
deliver *v.* 11
deserve *v.* 159
detention *n.* 165
diamond *n.* 84
die *v.* 40
diner *n.* 18
discover *v.* 14
discussion *n.* 159
disturb *v.* 112
dozen *adj.* 77
dream *n.* or *v.* 80
drown *v.* 150

E

earn *v.* 124
earring *n.* 55
earthquake *n.* 40
either . . . or *conj.* 124
elect *v.* 40
emphasize *v.* 128
encyclopedia *n.* 162
end *v.* or *n.* 156
enforce *v.* 165
engaged *adj.* 14
engagement *n.* 77
engineering *n.* 128
enough *adj, adv., or pron.* 18
entirely *adv.* 33
equator *n.* 14
eraser *n.* 165
even *adv.* 102
excited *adj.* 52
exercise *n.* or *v.* 30
expensive *adj.* 18

F

fair *adj.* 68
fancy *adj.* 96
fantastic *adj.* 55
far *adv.* 146
fault *n.* 134
feed *v.* 106
few *adj.* 14
finally *adv.* 18
find *v.* 14
fire *v.* 11
fireworks (plural) *n.* 46
fix *v.* 112
fresh *adj.* 30
friendly *adj.* 2
fun *n.* 30
furniture *n.* 99

G

gain *v.* or *n.* 71
gee *idiom* 77
geography *n.* 162
get *v.* 58
get *v.* 99
get used to *idiom* 80
go ahead *idiom* 27
go back *v.* 58
goal *n.* 33
goal *n.* 124
God *n.* 58
golden retriever *n.* 90
grade *n.* 128
grant *n.* 172
grateful *adj.* 58
groceries (plural) *n.* 124
grocery store *n.* 124
guess *v.* or *n.* 33
gum *n.* 165

H

Halloween *n.* 49
hard *adv.* or *adj.* 24
hate *v.* or *n.* 11
have got to *idiom* 5
have in common *idiom* 74
have to *idiom* 8
head *v.* or *n.* 58
help-wanted ad *n.* 14
hide *v.* 159
hill *n.* 137
hire *v.* 14
hit (base hit) *n.* 40
homework *n.* 24
honey *n.* 99
honeymoon *n.* 146
hop *v.* or *n.* 140
however *conj.* 40

humid *adj.* 14
hunt *v.* or *n.* 30
hurry *n.* or *v.* 124
hurt *v.* 27

I

ice hockey (often hockey) *n.*
 33
iceberg *n.* 146
imagine *v.* 2
immediately *adv.* 143
immigrant *n.* 18
importance *n.* 128
Independence Day *n.* 46
insist *v.* 106
institute *n.* 121
insurance *n.* 134
interfere *v.* 128

J

jealous *adj.* 68
join *v.* 46
join *v.* 84
joke *n.* or *v.* 102
jump *v.* or *n.* 106
just *adv.* 30
just *adv.* 71
just *adv.* 74
just *adv.* 168

K

kid *v.* 8
kid *n.* 36
kind *adj.* 62
knot *n.* 146

L

land *v.* or *n.* 58
language *n.* 124
last *adj.* 52
last *v.* 55
later *adv.* 5
laugh *v.* or *n.* 102
lazybones *n.* 162
let's = let us *v.* 99
letter carrier *n.* 11
lick *v.* or *n.* 90
lie *v.* or *n.* 134
lifeboat *n.* 150
lifeguard *n.* 128
like *prep.* 8
little by little *idiom* 172
load *v.* or *n.* 150
lonely *adj.* 80
lookout *n.* 150
lose *v.* 5
lottery *n.* 93
low *adj.* 2

lower *v.* 150
lucky *adj.* 24
luxury *n.* 146

M

Macy's *n.* 52
make sense *idiom* 96
mall *n.* 102
mark *n.* or *v.* 159
mashed potatoes *n.* 52
match *v.* or *n.* 71
match *v.* or *n.* 99
matchmaker *n.* 71
matter *v.* 77
me too *idiom* 49
mean *v.* 33
midnight *n.* 124
millionaire *n.* 71
mind *v.* 55
miss *v.* 18
mix *v.* 80
mood *n.* 115

N

nachos *n.* 118
neighborhood *n.* 124
news *n.* 33
news *n.* 102
next *adj.* 33
no longer *idiom* 84
no wonder *idiom* 165
noisy *adj.* 80
nonsense *n.* 115
not . . . at all *idiom* 106
notice *v.* 99

O

object *v.* 106
of course *idiom* 8
off *prep.* 40
old-fashioned *adj.* 77
on the way *idiom* 137
once *adv.* 33
once *adv.* 168
once in a while *idiom* 55
opportunity *n.* 80
outdoors *adv.* 11
over *prep.* 134
overweight *adj.* 102
own *adj.* or *v.* 58

P

pair *n.* 55
parade *n.* or *v.* 46
peaceful *adj.* 14
pediatrician *n.* 128
perfect *adj.* 36
pet *v.* 90

Pilgrims *n.* 58
pirate *n.* 49
plant *v.* or *n.* 58
pleased *adj.* 62
police officer *n.* 8
polite *adj.* 2
pool (swimming pool) *n.* 46
portable *adj.* 55
· pound *n.* 27
prefer *v.* 102
pretty *adv.* 143
probably *adv.* 115
promise *v.* or *n.* 168
propose *v.* 84
protect *v.* 62
proud (of) *adj.* 33
public *n.* or *adj.* 121
pumpkin *n.* 49
puppy *n.* 90

Q

quickly *adv.* 84
quit *v.* 93

R

real estate *n.* 71
relax *v.* 112
remind *v.* 18
report *n.* or *v.* 46
rescue *v.* or *n.* 150
respect *n.* or *v.* 172
retire *v.* 40
retire *v.* 137
ride *v.* or *n.* 137
rifle *n.* 30
room *n.* 140
roomy *adj.* 140
rough *adj.* 33
rug *n.* 99
rule *n.* or *v.* 165
rush *v.* or *n.* 11

S

sacrifice *n.* or *v.* 124
sail *v.* or *n.* 58
salsa *n.* 118
scar *n.* or *v.* 143
scholarship *n.* 172
score *v.* or *n.* 33
scout *n.* or *v.* 36
season *n.* 30
secret *n.* 77
section *n.* 146
secure *adj.* 11
senior *n.* 128
sense of humor *n.* 159
several *adj.* 146
ship *n.* or *v.* 58

shoot *v.* 30
show how *v.* 58
sign *v.* 36
silly *adj.* 33
since *conj.* 106
sink *v.* 150
skinny *adj.* 36
slip *v.* or *n.* 143
slow down *v.* 150
smile *n.* or *v.* 14
so *adv.* 5
so *conj.* 18
so *adv.* 74
so *conj.* 102
So? *idiom* 77
soccer *n.* 18
soon *adv.* 14
sorry *adj.* 5
sound *v.* 159
speed *v.* or *n.* 134
spend *v.* 93
spicy *adj.* 118
spirit *n.* 33
spy *n.* or *v.* 121
stand *v.* 118
standard *adj.* 140
star *n.* or *v.* 33
starve *v.* 112
stay *v.* or *n.* 62
steady *adj.* 168
still *adv.* 8
stitch *n.* or *v.* 143
stranger *n.* 90
strict *adj.* 172
such *adj.* 80
suddenly *adv.* 150
sugar cane *n.* 36
suggest *v.* 55
sunny *adj.* 46
supplies (plural) *n.* 40
surprise *n.* or *v.* 162
swimsuit *n.* 46

T

taco *n.* 118
Taco Bell *n.* 118
tail *n.* 106
take off *v.* or *n.* 40
teammate *n.* 36
terrible *adj.* 40
then *adv.* 115
throw *n.* or *v.* 36
ticket *n.* 93
tip *n.* or *v.* 2
tired *adj.* 24
tired of *adj.* 115
together *adv.* 52

too *adv.* 2
too *adv.* 24
tough *adj.* 2
train *v.* 121
treat *n.* or *v.* 49
trick *n.* or *v.* 49
trick or treat *idiom* 49
trouble *n.* 134
trunk *n.* 140
trust *n.* or *v.* 62
truth *n.* 134
turkey *n.* 52
type *n.* 71

U

understand *v.* 5
uniform *n.* 40
unsinkable *adj.* 150
upset *adj.* or *v.* 96

V

vacation *n.* 124
Valentine's Day *n.* 77
valuable *adj.* 40
vegetarian *n.* 102
veteran *n.* or *adj.* 146
view *n.* or *v.* 18
village *n.* 168
voyage *n.* 146

W

wag *v.* 106
waitress *n.* 2
warn *v.* 118
warning *n.* 146
waste *v.* or *n.* 93
wealthy *adj.* or *n.* 146
weigh *v.* 27
well *idiom* 68
What's the matter? *idiom* 96
whatever *pron.* 102
why *idiom* 2
willing *adj.* 74
win *v.* 93
wiz *n.* 128
wonderful *adj.* 52
woods (plural) *n.* 30
worry *v.* or *n.* 24
worse *adj.* 134
worship *v.* or *n.* 58
worth *prep.* or *n.* 140
wow *idiom* 156
wrong *adj.* 5

Y

yard *n.* 143
yell *v.* or *n.* 165
yet *adv.* 55